DUKE ELLINGTON
A LIFE OF MUSIC

DUKE ELLINGTON

A LIFE OF MUSIC

EVE STWERTKA

An Impact Biography

FRANKLIN WATTS
New York
Chicago
London
Toronto
Sydney

Photographs copyright ©:
The Duke Ellington Collection, Smithsonian
Institution: pp. 1, 2 top, 3, 9;
Wide World Photos: pp. 2 bottom, 14;
UPI/Bettmann Newsphotos: pp. 4 top, 5 top,
7, 15, 16; The Bettmann Archive: pp. 4 bottom,
5 bottom, 6, 8, 10 top; William P. Gottlieb: pp. 10 bottom
11, 12; Archive Photos: p. 13.

Library of Congress Cataloging-in-Publication Data

Stwertka, Eve.
Duke Ellington : a life of music / by Eve Stwertka.
p. cm.—(An Impact biography)
Includes bibliographical references (p.) and index.
ISBN 0-531-13035-5
1. Ellington, Duke, 1899–1974—Juvenile literature. 2. Jazz
musicians—United States—Biography—Juvenile literature.
[1. Ellington, Duke, 1899–1974. 2. Musicians. 3. Composers.
4. Afro-Americans—Briography.] I. Title.
ML3930.E44S79 1993
781.65'092—dc20
[B]   93-21267
CIP AC MN

CONTENTS

ACKNOWLEDGMENTS

The author is grateful to the following organizations for their help and courtesy:

The Schomburg Center for Research in Black Culture, New York City, and in particular the staff of the Department of Moving Image and Recorded Sound; the Spingarn Research Center of Howard University, Washington, D.C.; the Duke Ellington Society of New York; and Saint Peter's Church, in Manhattan, New York's spiritual jazz headquarters.

Special thanks go to Michael Cogswell for his expert reading of my manuscript. His valuable corrections and most of his suggestions for modification have been incorporated in this book.

CHAPTER ONE

JAZZ NEEDS NO PASSPORT

Turn on the radio in most places of the world, and you'll probably hear popular music with an American sound to it. It might be some form of jazz, blues, rock, country, or rap. The lyrics might be in a language you can't understand, but its roots will reach back to the U.S.A., where the African-American connection began.

From the start, jazz had a way of getting under people's skin. The African-inspired rhythms, the hesitations that lengthen out a beat, the softly liberated scale, were foreign to the Western ear. It was an alien sound, but yet familiar, like the excited thumping of one's heart, and at times a cross between a song and a cry. It was great music for dancing, but at the same time it could create an ache of longing.

The agitated sounds of jazz suited the restless spirit of the twentieth century perfectly. Gradually, it edged out the popular music that had originated in the European countries. Sounds of accordions, bagpipes and strings, the lilt of waltzes, polkas, and tangos, gave way to the more elemental drive of the African beat from across the ocean.

The music known as jazz had originated in the work songs of African slaves in the American South. Minstrel shows were popular in the nineteenth century, with their plantation-style singing, dancing, and banjo playing by black performers or by white imitators in blackface. After the Civil War, many black marching bands adopted brass instruments, adding yet another element to the mix of sounds. As the newly freed people migrated north, their music moved with them. In the 1920s, blues and jazz spread beyond the black community. Professionally trained musicians discovered black music. Writers of Broadway musicals and composers of concert symphonies adapted it. Young people of all ethnic backgrounds were captivated by it. Jazz permeated their dancing and life-styles so that the decade after World War I came to be called the Jazz Age. On both sides of the Atlantic, people clamored for the new strains and rhythms.

Growing up in the early twentieth century, Duke Ellington fell in quite naturally with the birth of the new music. One could say jazz carried him to the top, except that it was really the other way around. It was he, the great American musician, who helped to move jazz upward from its humble start. Yet he had this to say about it to his audiences:

You probably heard of the word "jazz." It's all right if that is the way you understand or prefer it. We stopped using the word in 1943, and we much prefer to call it the American Idiom, or the Music of Freedom of Expression.[1]

When the African artist Papa Tall asked Duke to explain jazz, Duke compared it to a wonderful tree. Its roots, he said, are firmly planted in "the rich black earth of beautiful Black Africa," while its branches reach out in all directions—east, west, and north. The blossoms of the tree come out in all sizes, shapes, and colors, and the fruits are just as varied. There isn't any place on earth where people can't reach that tree and enjoy it.[2] Jazz, in its many forms, has traveled far and freely without needing a passport.

As pianist, composer, bandleader, show business genius, nonstop performer, and ambassador of cool for his country, Ellington promoted his native folk music. He escorted it from the little back-alley bars where he first found it, all the way to the concert halls and courts and cathedrals throughout the world. Duke liked to say, "Music is my mistress," and when he came to write his autobiography, he used this affectionate statement for the title of his book. He also once gave a friend his definition of music: "Mass unity sounding in concert—M-U-S-I-C."[3]

Ellington was born into a historical period that was ready to welcome his art, and he was the first to acknowledge his good fortune. At the height of his career, he had this to say in introducing one of his sacred music concerts:

As I travel from place to place by car, bus, train, plane . . . taking rhythm to the dancers, harmony to the romantic, melody to the nostalgic, gratitude to the listener . . . receiving praise, applause, and handshakes, and at the same time doing the thing I like to do, I feel that I am most fortunate because I know that God has blessed my timing, without which no thing could have happened—the right time or place or with the right people. The four must converge. Thank God.[4]

Among Duke's contemporaries there were other great music makers. Some were wonderful instrumentalists, others were gifted singers, still others composed memorable songs. But none gave such original music so consistently to the public over such a long period of time.

When Duke Ellington died in 1974, ten thousand mourners filled the Cathedral of St. John the Divine in

11

New York City where the funeral took place. Another twenty-five hundred fans stood outside. The *New York Times*, in its front-page report, went so far as to call him "America's most important composer."[5] Setting aside the importance of Duke the musician, though, blues vocalist Sarah Vaughan reminisced about Duke the man. "He has made us all happier and richer by having lived among us," she said. "He will not be easily replaced on this earth."[6]

CHAPTER TWO

A CHARMED CIRCLE

Edward Kennedy Ellington, later known to the world as "Duke," was born in Washington, D.C., on April 29, 1899. At first, his young parents and their baby stayed in the Kennedy grandparents' house with its spacious garden. Later, they settled on T Street between 11th and 12th Streets, and this is where Duke Ellington remembers spending most of his childhood.

T Street hasn't changed very much over the years. The two- or three-story homes look inviting, with tiny front yards and ornamental iron staircases, southern-style. The block is still part of a pleasant, black ethnic neighborhood of wide tree-lined streets.

Edward had so many relatives on both sides of his family that all of Washington was his domain. There were aunts, uncles, and cousins to be visited in every part of town. The center of action, though, was still the home of his Kennedy grandparents where wonderful "Mamma" ruled supreme. The Kennedys had raised ten children—five boys and five girls. Even after the daughters were married, they flocked back to Mamma's house bringing their youngsters, whom Mamma fed and pampered and treated as one enormous family. Edward and his five girl cousins romped in Mamma's backyard, chased the family dogs, climbed the pear trees, or rested under the grape arbor.

One of Edward's earliest memories was of running

to examine his grandmother's rosebushes, falling, and cutting his finger. That year he also developed pneumonia. His mother, who nursed him night and day, was in despair when she found him too sick to speak to her. He recalls that she sat by his bedside for hours, sometimes kneeling to pray, and sometimes leaning over him and crying, "My own child doesn't even recognize me!"

A powerful bond of devotion between mother and son formed very early and remained strong throughout their lives. They truly idolized one another. Duke's mother, the former Daisy Kennedy, was delicately beautiful, with luminous dark eyes, pale skin, and fine features. Her father, James William Kennedy, had been a police captain, with a good steady income and some social standing in the community.

Daisy cared deeply about respectability and refined manners. Above all, she was devoutly religious. She used to take her son to two different churches every Sunday, and tell him delightful stories about God. Naturally, she sent him to Sunday school. When Edward started going to regular school, she followed him to school and back again, keeping her distance and trying not to let him see her. Protective as she was, she must have been tactful, too, for instead of rebelling, her son accepted her assurances that he was very, very special. She would say to him, "Edward, you are blessed. You don't have anything to worry about. Edward, you are blessed!"[1]

Even though Washington was a strictly segregated city in those days, Daisy Ellington did not permit any sense of discrimination to reach her son. In later years, Ellington could not remember when he first became aware of racial differences. "There was never any talk about red people, brown people, black people, or yellow people," he recalled.[2] Instead, he thought his mother's idea about the Creation must have been that

"God took some rich black soil, some red clay, and some white sand, and mixed them all together to make the first man, so that forever after no man would feel he was better than another."[3] The story makes good sense in the light of the Kennedy family background that included a combination of African, European, and Native American ancestors.[4]

Duke's father, James Edward Ellington, or "J.E." as people called him, was an alert and enterprising man. After he and his brothers moved to Washington from North Carolina, in the 1890s, he worked as a waiter and a coachman, before he was promoted to the steady job of butler in the family of Dr. M. F. Cuthburt, a successful, white society doctor. Later, J.E. managed his own boardinghouse and catering service, and then became a blueprint-maker for the United States Navy.

J.E. aspired to live like a gentleman, and he tried to raise his family "as though he were a millionaire."[5] Although he was probably fairly well paid, an extra job was always welcome. Now and then he helped out at social functions around town—even at the White House, it is said—and sometimes, when Dr. Cuthburt was giving a large party, Daisy, too, went along to lend a hand.

As butler in a well-appointed household, J.E. was put in charge of other servants and saw to it that everything was kept running smoothly. He was quick to learn about the best brands of china and crystal, the finest cuts of meat, and the highest quality of game. He cultivated a flowery way of speaking and was something of a sweet talker, especially with women, as he was inordinately fond of the opposite sex even to the end of his days.

J.E. liked everything done with style and regularity. At home, he planned the dinner menu for the week. Duke recalled that on Sundays they could always

15

count on having baked chicken and macaroni and cheese. Wednesdays, it was ham with baked beans and kale, while Thursdays, it was usually a fine, aromatic stew. Tuesday was surprise day, when Daisy used her imagination. She served up leftovers with the skill and dash of an artist, and made the world's best corn bread.

Until his sister, Ruth, was born sixteen years later, Duke enjoyed all the privileges of an only child. He remembers teaching his little sister to walk by holding onto her pigtails, a game she enjoyed but his mother frowned on. By the time Ruth was born, though, Duke was old enough to be married himself.

Meanwhile, he grew up sheltered by a large, loving family, supported by his mother's conviction that he was blessed, and certain that large and small pleasures would come around with perfect regularity, just like the chicken dinner after church on Sundays. Father and mother watched over him, and his grandparents were always nearby. Affectionate uncles, aunts, and cousins—both Kennedys and Ellingtons—lived within easy reach. In short, Duke grew up in a charmed circle of warmth and affection that made him feel safe and confident. As he liked to say in later life, "If I couldn't be Duke, I'd rather be the son of my father and mother."[6]

Although young Edward was lucky enough to be protected from racial prejudice, life was far more harsh for many other black Americans. The memory of slavery and the Civil War still rankled. Besides the physical and economic devastation they caused, slavery and war had left spiritual scars on black people. True, the Civil War had been won by the Northern states, and with the passing of the Thirteenth Amendment in 1865, slavery had been abolished once and for all. During the post-war Reconstruction period, the federal government passed new laws to prevent the former slaveholding states from backsliding. In 1866, a civil rights act was passed by both houses of Congress, at last conferring citizenship on blacks. And with citizenship came equal rights to enjoy the benefit of all laws.

Although this prevented the South from reverting to outright slavery, individual states and local governments, nevertheless, passed a long list of so-called Jim Crow laws that discriminated against people of color and segregated them from other Americans. The laws left the African-American citizen few rights and little freedom. In public and in private, segregated areas kept the two races apart. Blacks had to live in certain parts of town and go to separate schools and churches. They could not enter hotels and restaurants except as servants. They were forced to sit in the rear section of buses. When traveling from north to south on the railroad, black people had to move to separate compartments as soon as the trains crossed the Mason-Dixon line. Even public waiting rooms, washrooms, and drinking fountains forced customers to use separate facilities marked "colored" and "white." In addition to the constant insult of such rules, the Jim Crow laws were also applied to employment and wages. And anyone who disobeyed these laws was sent to prison.

Furthermore, the dreaded Ku Klux Klan, which was dedicated to reestablishing white supremacy, had been founded in Tennessee at the end of the Civil War. Its membership which extended throughout the South, made anti-black riots, mob killings, and house burnings common occurrences. The horror of lynching remained unabated well into the twentieth century. The year Duke Ellington was born, 85 black people were lynched, a relatively low number compared to the 101 lynchings the year before in 1898, and the 105 that took place the following year in 1900.[7]

Not only did black people live in constant fear but

few jobs were open to them, and they had to endure poverty, illiteracy, segregated schools, and miserable housing. As a result, thousands of black people left the former slaveholding states and moved north in search of work and a better life. Many of them succeeded, but others came to grief in miserable conditions. In those years, even laborers and domestic servants had trouble finding work, because they were competing with the millions of immigrants from foreign countries pouring into the United States, hungry for the same employment.

Immigrants and blacks competed not only for jobs but for housing, causing friction between the different ethnic groups. To make things worse, many bosses would replace striking white workers with black strikebreakers who equally needed work. In spite of such obstacles, however, African-Americans were able to move steadily forward.

The beginning of a new century tends to make people believe that change for the better is coming. Duke Ellington's family was no exception. The District of Columbia held a special attraction for families like the Kennedys and the Ellingtons. Black families moved to Washington, D.C., from many southern states after emancipation from bondage gave them the right to choose where to live. To go north had long meant to find freedom, and the city of Washington lay in the right direction, yet still close enough to the South to be familiar in climate and customs. Above all, the District of Columbia was the seat of the government that had decreed the freedom of the black people. In Washington blacks could hold political office and in 1867 the federal government founded Howard University, in the northwest part of the city, as a college specifically designed for black students.

At the turn of the century, when little Edward Ellington was a toddler, 86,702 black people lived in Washington, D.C.[8] Not all families who moved there were as successful as the Kennedys and the Ellingtons. Behind the rows of splendid mansions occupied by wealthy whites, poor black people lived in alleys filled with stench and filth. Much of the city was built on swampland, without proper sanitation and sewage facilities. Lacking both water and drainage, the shacks of the poorest of the poor were hovels planted helter-skelter in mud.

As a result, a strong sense of social differences arose in the black community of the city. In fact, there was a kind of caste system, with a great deal of pride among those black people near the top. Duke Ellington writes in his memoirs, "I don't know how many castes of Negroes there were in the city at that time, but I do know that if you decided to mix carelessly with another, you would be told that one just did not do that sort of thing."[9]

Clearly, Ellington had no trouble considering himself a member of the upper crust. His manner was charming, though a little shy, and he was basically self-confident. In a picture taken at the age of four, he stands proudly in a neat little military outfit with brass buttons. In later years, he continued to enjoy dressing well. It's easy to see why, at some time during his school career, Edward Kennedy Ellington acquired the name "Duke." The aristocratic title stuck with him through life.

Duke's school was segregated, and since it was in a black middle-class neighborhood, it was resolutely conservative. At one point, parents and teachers opposed the proposal to integrate with a white school because the white kids who would come in would have been socially unacceptable to them.

The school stressed knowledge of "Negro His-

19

tory," and pride in the African-American heritage. It also placed strong emphasis on good speech and manners. According to Duke, Miss Boston, the principal, told them to remember that out in the wider world they would be observed and judged as representatives of their race. They would always be "onstage."

When Mrs. Ellington at last permitted her son Edward to venture beyond the neighborhood, she made sure he was accompanied by his older cousin, Sonny Ellington. The two boys would walk the long distance to the wilderness of Rock Creek Park. Often they spent their carfare on snacks and candy, so they had to trudge back home again, too. Along the way, they might stop at an aunt or uncle's house. These relatives were all great bakers, who liked nothing better than to stuff the youngsters with pies and cookies, or homemade ice cream and fresh fruit. No wonder Duke later wrote a whole chapter on "The Taste Buds" in his autobiography!

Sonny was a good athlete. Among other things, he tried to teach Duke how to swim—but in vain. Both boys liked to read adventure stories, and Duke quickly made his way through Sonny's huge collection of pulp Westerns and detective stories.

In this period drugs were practically unknown in the black middle classes, and young people didn't carry knives or guns. Groups of boys played baseball in vacant lots and on an abandoned tennis court at Sixteenth Street. Sometimes, President Theodore Roosevelt would ride by on horseback and stop to watch them for a while. When he rode on, the boys would wave to him. If you can imagine the president of the United States taking a leisurely stroll through town, without armored cars or bodyguards, you will understand the comparative innocence of those days.

This innocence also extended to the way people

entertained themselves in their spare time. The technological marvels of radio, film, and television had not yet been invented. Only the very rich had electric lights, a telephone, or an automobile. But music was beloved by everyone, and in almost every middle-class home at least one person played the piano. People liked to crowd around the piano and sing the folk songs and hymns that were popular at the time. Daisy Ellington had taken piano lessons and played very nicely, while her husband played tunes by ear.

Wanting to give their son all the advantages of a good education, the Ellingtons sent him to a neighborhood teacher for piano lessons. Appropriately, her name was Mrs. Clinkscales. The Ellingtons paid Mrs. Clinkscales for many lessons, but Duke had no tolerance for sitting still and practicing. Often he kept Mrs. Clinkscales waiting, or ran off to play and didn't show up at all.

Duke didn't give Mrs. Clinkscales a chance to teach him music. This man who would perform so brilliantly later was not a very devoted student. He did not even finish high school. Asked about this as an adult, Ellington commented, "I've always felt that a man's education doesn't start until he finds out what he wants to learn. And then you know what to learn."[10]

In school, his best subject was art. He liked to draw and paint, and work with colors. Seeing that their son had genuine talent, his parents encouraged him, and in the light of this new activity they allowed him to drop his piano lessons. For a while, it looked as if Duke were preparing himself for a career in the visual arts.

Music critics and biographers often point out the visual elements in Ellington's music. James Lincoln Collier writes that one of Duke's "greatest strengths as a composer" is his "rich tone palette," his "shifts of color," while Derek Jewell comments on the number

21

of Duke's compositions that feature colors in their titles.[11]

For the moment, high school was preparing Duke
for a career as an artist. No one had an inkling that
the youth would soon turn his talents in an unexpected
direction.

CHAPTER THREE

HOOKED ON MUSIC

Before the days of air conditioning, summers in sweltering Washington could be quite an ordeal. While fathers of families were forced to stay on the job and sweat it out, those who could afford it sent their wives and children to the seashore. Part of J.E.'s idea of "living like a millionaire" was to make sure Daisy and Edward spent every summer out of the city. They would stay either with an aunt in Atlantic City or with an uncle in Philadelphia. Young Edward was thrilled by these trips and always loved the adventure of traveling in a Pullman parlor car.

One summer, Daisy chose to go to Asbury Park, New Jersey, a popular beach resort on the Atlantic Ocean. Duke, about to enter high school, was reaching the age when pocket money is always in short supply. So, while his mother took her vacation, he landed a job as dishwasher in a small hotel in Asbury Park.

With his talent for making friends wherever he went, Edward immediately found a pal, a young fellow named Bowser, who was working as the headwaiter. Bowser took pity on the inexperienced newcomer and washed most of the dishes for him. The two boys had lots of time to chat. Edward told Bowser how much he enjoyed hearing good piano playing, and Bowser was enthusiastic about a terrific young pianist named Harvey Brooks, just then working in Philadelphia. At the

23

end of the summer, the boys went to hear Brooks play. Edward was bowled over by Brooks's swinging rhythms and "tremendous left hand."[1] Without knowing the name for it then, Edward apparently was hearing some really good "stride" piano playing.

By the time he returned to Washington, Edward was on fire to master the keyboard. True, the genteel tinkle of the keys heard in Mrs. Clinkscales's parlor hadn't made much of an impression on him. But now he was hearing a different sort of piano playing. It had a strutting, cheeky beat that made one want to dance. It combined the elements of "ragtime" and "blues," two forms of music that had been born in the black South, but were rapidly making their way across America. Ragtime is ninety-nine percent the pianist's domain and the term "stride" refers exclusively to piano playing.

Only a few players had the knack for doing the stride. While the left hand walked, stalked, and jumped along the keys of the bass, the right hand flew back and forth higher up, playing another melody. The two hands cavorted like a pair of dancers, separate and yet together.

Like ragtime and blues, stride had a driving rhythm spiced with syncopation—a hesitation in the rhythm, slightly off the beat. Syncopation has a thrilling quality, like feeling one's heart skip a beat in a moment of excitement. Like many "offbeat" experiences, it has the element of surprise.

The traditional music of white Americans came from Europe. In European music, the rhythm tends to be highly regular with the emphasis on the downbeat, and syncopation used sparingly. Suddenly, a new African-American sound was introducing an element of the unexpected. It placed a startling stress on the beats that are normally unaccented. It made the rhythm seem ragged. Hearing this "ragging" of the beat, people began calling the music Ragtime.

Actually, as jazz critic James Lincoln Collier notes, early ragtime music did not use simple, European-style syncopation.[2] Instead the music was based on the extremely complicated cross-rhythms of African drumming and percussion music. Drumming, an ancient tradition in African villages, is not just an entertainment but a kind of language and religious observance. Above all, it is functional, often marking the time of day or time of eating. African drumming is so highly developed that groups of drummers can play with—and against—one another, "crossing" their different rhythms without interfering. A drummer can even play two entirely different rhythms at the same time, each with one hand. This is polyrhythmic. (To see how hard this is, try rapping the table three times with one hand while giving it four taps with the other.)

The stride piano players used the technique of cross-rhythms in their music. They had a way of holding or rushing the beat, doing what came naturally at the moment, and creating a new sound that was hard to imitate.

Ragtime sprang also from the sounds of the American banjo and the marching band. The banjo is a descendant of the West African musical instrument, *les*, and was first played by African slaves. Piano players introduced it in brothels and bars, and traveling shows. At first, it carried a whiff of lowlife that was alien to strictly respectable folks such as Edward's family. His mother, who could read music, played hymns and sweetly sentimental songs, while J.E. improvised melodies from classical opera by ear. Middle-class people like the Ellingtons did not care for blues and ragtime. Both sounded coarse to them.

Although many performers played ragtime by ear,

the best-known composer of "rags," Scott Joplin (1868–1917), had formal musical training. A serious musician, Joplin wrote down and published his compositions, and it was partly through his work that ragtime gained a measure of respectability. In any case, for the younger generation, black and white alike, this music was heady, liberating stuff. Edward and his friends were wild about it.

For the moment, Edward's piano lessons and his parents' musical tastes were more of a hindrance than a help. His background had attuned his ear to European-American music, and not to cross-rhythms, ragged beats, or other sounds of African origin. Of course, much ragtime sheet music was available at the time, but in his impatience Edward had not learned to read notes. Hard as he tried, he couldn't become a dazzling piano player. Though he later developed a style of understated elegance uniquely his own, he was not one of those rare natural geniuses who take to the keyboard as if they were born to play.

It was in high school that Edward discovered a new side of big-city life in Washington. He had only to walk along T Street to the block between Sixth and Seventh, to find himself in front of the Howard Theater, Washington's leading showcase for black performers. Next door, in Frank Holliday's poolroom, he could catch a glimpse of Washington's most successful black men, as well as others who were part of the city's underworld.

Today, the Howard Theater stands empty, and the yellow brick building next to it, with the faded sign reading BILLIARDS, is bolted. Both structures, monuments to African-American's past history, deserve restoration. When Ellington was in his teens, Frank Holliday's poolroom drew elite crowds, even from outside the District of Columbia. Here, black musicians would drop in, sit down casually at the piano, and let fly with their latest techniques. These were men who had been to St. Louis, Kansas City, Chicago, or New York. They didn't just repeat the popular ragtime tunes that were currently available on printed sheet music and, after many repetitions, could sound stiff and mechanical. Rather, they let their fingers follow their imagination. Their music came to them from sounds heard, perhaps, in childhood: field-workers' shouts, street vendors' cries, marching bands, and hymns sung in church. They also incorporated the music of other great piano players that they had heard in their travels. After the show at the Howard Theater next door, musicians—trumpeters, guitarists, drummers—would drop in to the poolroom. The players would show off, trying to top one another in "cutting contests," while everyone stopped by to listen. The musicians would cheer one another on and learn from each other's performance.

Frank Holliday's poolroom was strictly off-limits to kids, but Duke and his pals gained admission by pretending to be sixteen. The place offered the newcomer plenty to stare at—and overhear. Great pool sharks, from all over town, mingled with gamblers, cardsharps, even pickpockets proud of their nimble fingers. But there were also students from nearby Howard University—future doctors and lawyers, as well as Pullman porters and dining-car waiters—men who traveled back and forth across the country and could tell a good story. The air was thick with cigar smoke, the hum of voices, the clicking of billiard balls—and there was always someone having a go at the piano.

Just as enticing for a boy in his early teens was the Gaiety, a vaudeville and variety theater, where women also did the striptease on stage. A small band usually accompanied the different acts, which featured dancing, singing, acrobatics, and comedy teams. Variety theater had to keep a restless audience

27

constantly amused. Ellington was impressed with the timing, staging, and costumes. These were his first lessons in theater and showmanship, for which he later demonstrated a natural flair. At the same time, of course, he didn't exactly turn his eyes away from the good-looking strippers in various stages of undress.

Edward had noticed that women seemed to be drawn to musicians. As soon as someone sat down at the piano, one or two young girls would appear as if by magic, lean against the piano top, and follow his every move with admiring eyes. More than ever, Edward was determined to play. He tried once again to learn the basics from some of the pianists he met, and master the stride style of playing, making his left hand sound as if someone were stalking up and down the keyboard in giant steps. But, still, he couldn't get the hang of it.

One week, however, Edward came down with a bad cold. Home from school and from his soda-fountain job at the Poodle Dog Café, he spent hours at the piano, trying to fit together everything he had ever learned. This time his persistence paid off. He picked his way around the keys until he actually put together a passable ragtime composition, which he called "Soda Fountain Rag." The more he played it, the more he felt at ease. Soon, he went on to compose his second rag, "What You Gonna Do When the Bed Breaks Down?" He remembers that it featured "a pretty good 'hug-and-rubbin' 'crawl,'"[3] which reveals that he was developing technique as well as composing skill. He didn't know it then, but his famous musical career was off to a start.

With their catchy titles, Edward's compositions made quite a hit among the high-school crowd. One of his classmates insisted on crashing a party held by seniors and getting Ellington to play for them. The older students were so delighted that they instantly "promoted" the youngster to senior rank by taking him out for blackberry wine with gin, a concoction they called Top and Bottom. It was also around this time that his friends promoted him to superior rank by bestowing on him the title of "Duke."

As a result of his sudden fame, three pretty young girls came by one morning to pick up the young musician on his way to school. Or so they said, anyway. As soon as they were all around the corner, though, the girls told him that they would all be going to someone's house instead. There would be music, they said, and they were going to "have a hop."

Along with ragtime, a new style of dancing was becoming the latest craze. The new music and the new dance steps were made for one another. In the nineteenth century, ballroom dancing had been a rare and special occasion. The young girls always arrived with a chaperone, and behaved with decorum. Formal dancing usually required couples to keep changing partners, and even when partners faced one another and touched hands, they didn't hold one another close.

In the new dances, couples gripped one another in a bear hug and trotted around the room, with the man usually walking his partner backward. One can tell that ragtime grew out of marching-band music. Its jigging beat invited a kind of exaggerated walk. Many of the dances were called "trots" or "shuffles." Actually, a theatrical forerunner of these dances, the Cake Walk, had been a minstrel-show favorite before the Civil War.

Suddenly, everyone wanted to dance. People went dancing in the afternoons and evenings. They danced in restaurants, bars, hotels, rented halls, one another's homes, and, of course, in high-school gymnasiums. So a piano player, or, better still, a band was always needed. This dance craze, which changed the entire courting and dating pattern of young people in America, continued through the first half of the twentieth century, until the end of the Second World War. Much later in life, Duke Ellington would become a composer of serious concert music, but it was the dance craze of his youth that gave his career its start. An early Ellington dance hit was "Doing the New Low-Down."

Meeting the musicians who played in the dance halls, theaters, and pool parlors was Duke's apprenticeship. He observed, listened, and fearlessly asked for instruction. Some of the great players who passed through town were glad to help the eager, polite young fellow. Some of these men were self-taught and couldn't read music; others had had formal conservatory training. Duke called them "the ear cats" and "the schooled guys" or "the Conservatory Boys." All of them were learning from one another.

Outstanding among the trained musicians was Oliver "Doc" Perry, a fine-looking, dignified man, whose beautifully groomed hands moved over the keys with ease. Along with his dexterity, Doc Perry knew a great deal about harmony and general music theory. He was evidently a good teacher and a generous person. He recognized Duke's talent, and invited him to visit whenever he liked. Duke came over almost every day, and Perry taught him to read the lead, or melodic line, of a piece of music, and recognize the chord structure. Doc Perry never charged his pupil a cent for all he taught him. On the contrary, he gave the youngster food and drink all day long. "How does one pay off this kind of indebtedness?" Duke asks in his autobiography. "[Doc Perry] was my piano parent."[4]

When word got around that young Ellington was showing talent, a second mentor, Henry Grant, entered his life. A well-known musician around Washington and the leader of an African-American Folk Song chorus. Grant had received formal training and now taught music at Duke's high school, Armstrong Tech. Like Perry, Grant invited Duke to drop in for informal lessons in harmony. With both teachers, unfortunately, Duke avoided studying written composition. As he would continue to do, he preferred talking over the music to writing it down.

This method served him well up to a point, but it had limitations. For one thing, it meant picking up a new piece the hard way—sometimes even from listening to a mechanical player piano. Player pianos were very popular until they were replaced by record players and radios. Inside a player piano is a roll of paper on which holes representing notes of music have been punched out. As the paper roll unwinds, a mechanism inside the piano makes the keys move in response to the holes in the paper. Many of the great ragtime tunes were available on paper rolls, and people would rush to the stores to buy the latest ones.

Duke tells of going to a friend's house to hear a fabulous tune on a piano roll. It was "Carolina Shout" composed by the great James P. Johnson. As soon as he heard it, Duke knew he had to have it in his repertory, and he returned day after day to memorize it. While his friend slowed down the mechanical action of the piano, Duke painstakingly memorized the movement of the keys, until he could finally play "Carolina Shout" from start to finish.

All this hard work stood him in good stead. When James P. Johnson came in person to play at Washington's Convention Hall, a large cheering section of Duke's well-wishers pushed their buddy forward to perform "Carolina Shout" for the visiting composer. The older man praised Duke and invited him to act as his guide around the city's "hot spots." The two stayed out until ten o'clock the next morning. They remained friends, and Johnson was later to be a great help to Duke in New York.

Duke was still enrolled in the art program at Armstrong Technical High School, and showing a clear aptitude for commercial art. But the excitement of making music was exerting a strong pull on him. Piano players or small bands were in constant demand. Besides all the dances, there were social gatherings at which people liked having music played softly in the background. This was called "under conversation" music because once people started talking among themselves, they were hardly aware of the pianist. Even though Duke was inexperienced, some of the older players would send him out on jobs they were too busy to handle. At first, Duke knew so few pieces that he played the same ones over and over, but it hardly mattered. He developed a trick of throwing his hands way up in the air—a bit of showmanship he copied from a pianist he had seen at the Howard Theater. It looked dramatic and professional, and people kept asking for him when they needed some pleasant background sounds for their parties.

One day, a manager who had hired him before, sent Ellington to play at a ritzy country club. "Collect a hundred dollars and bring me ninety," the man said. That night, alone at the piano and playing nonstop, Duke had something to think about. Ten dollars out of a hundred! Why not act as his own manager? After he handed over the man's ninety dollars, Duke went to the telephone company and took out a large ad for himself in the phone book, under the section for "Musicians."

America was involved in World War I at this time. While the fighting raged in Europe, the capital of the United States was full of politicians, diplomats, and businessmen. Meetings and conferences went on around the clock, as well as receptions, cocktail parties, and Red Cross dances. Duke Ellington was too young to be drafted, but not too young to play piano in public, yet another instance of his being in the right place at the right time.

Although Duke was enjoying himself and making good money for a boy of his age, serious responsibilities were about to fall upon him. He and his longtime friend Edna Thompson had gone all through school together, but recently their friendship had turned to romance. In July of 1918, Duke and Edna were married, and in 1919 their son, Mercer, was born. A second child followed less than a year later, but did not survive. Reminiscing about her early marriage, Edna recalled, "We were very young, then. Kids, really. I think we both thought Mercer was a toy."[5]

Luckily, there was no shortage of work for Mercer's dad. The demand for music was tremendous, and he received plenty of calls in response to his advertisements. He organized several bands from among his circle of friends, sent them out to play at night, and often did some playing himself.

Practical and enterprising as he was, Duke and a partner also started a small sign-painting business on T Street, close to the Howard Theater. Making posters for dances now gave him a chance to learn about opportunities for his bands. On the other hand, if someone called with a booking for a band, he'd offer to make the advertising posters for the occasion as well. Occasionally he painted scenery at the Howard. "I had real good business sense then," he says in his memoirs.[6]

During his senior year at Armstrong High, Ellington won the prize in a poster contest sponsored by the NAACP—the prize, a scholarship to Pratt Institute in New York City. Pratt, a school renowned for its courses in commercial art, would have given him excellent

33

training and a good start in the commercial-art world. But with a young family to support, Ellington could hardly become a full-time student for the next four years. He was compelled to refuse the chance. Besides, when his senior year in high school came to an end, he failed to graduate. Apparently, he was one course short of the number required for a degree.

Early parenthood, plus lack of a high-school diploma, plus lack of formal professional training—this formula has spelled disaster for many a young man or woman. Indeed, biographer James Lincoln Collier believes that these difficult circumstances practically drove Duke Ellington into a musical career.

In those days, playing in music halls and dance halls was a specialty of African-Americans, for whom most other professions remained closed. The bands tended to be merely groups called together for a particular job. Work was plentiful and provided quick cash in a man's pockets, although socially, musical entertainers were low on the totem pole, classed on the level of servants and waiters.[7] As yet, the music they performed carried little prestige and promised no future. Still, Duke was happy to be earning enough to buy a car and provide housing for his wife and child.

Music had a hold on him for good, but he was not yet aware of it. It would be many years before he could put it into words: "So you're hooked on music. You think and anticipate music. You write music, play music, and listen to music. Your joy is music. You are lucky to be hooked on something you make a living by playing—and playing with—day after day, play after play, fifty-two weeks a year. . . ."[8]

Duke also belonged to a group that played together regularly at True Reformers Hall. The three Miller brothers, sons of a music teacher at Armstrong Tech formed the nucleus of the group. Between them, the brothers played saxophone, guitar, and drums. They were joined by Otto ("Toby") Hardwick, a neighborhood boy five years younger than Duke. Toby started out playing string bass, and when he first joined the group, he was still so small that his father had to carry his huge instrument. Soon, Toby switched to saxophone and then alto saxophone. Later, he moved to New York with Duke, where his sweet, smooth tone became an asset to the Ellington band.

Another early associate of Duke, who came and went for years, was trumpet player Arthur Whetsol. He had formal musical training, which made him one of the rare good readers among so many self-taught players. Arthur, a Seventh-Day Adventist, was very religious, proper, and well-spoken. He was a premedical student at Howard University, and although he eventually left the band to go back to school, he returned to perform with it several times. Whetsol's playing, says Duke, in his exuberant way of writing, was "sweet, but not syrupy, nor schmaltzy, nor surrealistic, it had a superiority of extrasensory dimensions."[9]

The flashiest member of Duke's early group was sharp-dressing, slick-talking drummer Sonny Greer. Duke relates affectionately that instead of following in his father's footsteps to become an electrical engineer, Sonny wasted his New Jersey childhood "bimbanging" on his mother's pots and pans. Greer was no mere drummer, but an inspired percussionist, who worked with an awesome array of equipment, including chimes, gongs, tympani, cymbals, tom-toms, snare drums, and bass drums, and had a knack for getting all kinds of "crazy effects."[10] Sonny and Duke took an immediate shine to each other, and Duke called Sonny "the nearest thing I ever had to a brother."[11]

Sonny Greer had been to New York, which gave him a special aura. The traveling showmen who came

35

through Washington depicted New York as the center of sophistication and excitement. At the time, the area called Harlem in the northern part of Manhattan was developing into a black ethnic neighborhood. African-Americans could get housing there, and jobs were available, too, as the end of World War I promised an economic boom. Like a magnet, Harlem drew people from the southern farmlands as well as from the big towns—Washington, St. Louis, Kansas City, and Chicago.

The attraction of Harlem was not lost on Duke Ellington and his friends. It filled their imagination. "We were awed," he writes, "by the never-ending roll of great talents there, talents in so many fields, in society music and blues, in vaudeville and songwriting, in jazz and theater, in dancing and comedy."[12]

Finally, Sonny Greer, the nerviest member of the group, wrangled them a job in New York. They would accompany a vaudeville performer named Wilbur Sweatman, whose act consisted of playing three clarinets at the same time. Duke moved Edna and Mercer to his parents' house, while he and his pals traveled to the "Big Apple," where they accompanied Sweatman onstage for a few days. But soon Sweatman was out of work, and the rest of them were broke.

Luckily, Sonny was a champion billiard player. The boys would hang around the poolroom until Sonny had won two dollars, then they would buy something to eat and make the rounds of the cabarets where the great musicians were appearing. They introduced themselves to piano players like James P. Johnson, Fats Waller, and Willie "The Lion" Smith. The Lion was especially supportive. He liked their clean appearance and polite manners. Once, he even gave Duke fifty cents to get himself a haircut.

Unfortunately, the group was unable to find

enough steady work to support itself. At last, the story goes, Duke found fifteen dollars in the street. "Then," he says, "we had a square meal, got on the train, and went back to Washington to get ourselves together before we tried it again."[13]

CHAPTER FOUR

BEAUTIFUL CATS AND GORGEOUS CHICKS

In spring of 1923, Fats Waller came to Washington to play piano for a burlesque show at the Gaiety theater. The show was going on to New York, but Waller was bored with it and making plans for a change. Duke Ellington, Sonny Greer, and Toby Hardwick couldn't listen enough to Waller's famous stride bass playing and gravelly voice. Fats, in turn, wanted to help these nice kids eager for a bite of the Big Apple. "Why don't you all come up to New York and take the job?" he said. "I'll tell 'em about you."[1]

The boys didn't hesitate for a moment. While Sonny and Toby went on ahead, Duke saw to it that Edna and Mercer were settled once again with his parents. A few days later he followed, traveling in style, as usual. After all, wasn't a good job waiting for him in the Big Apple? He rode in the parlor car, ate an expensive dinner on the train, grabbed a cab at Pennsylvania Station, and left the driver a big tip.

Alas, by the time he reached his friends, he was broke. Not only that. The job had evaporated and they were broke, too. Again, Willie "The Lion" Smith took them under his wing, and other musicians helped them by letting the boys sit in on their gigs and splitting the tips with them. All his life, Duke would meet up with "beautiful cats" like these—generous men willing to give support and advice and kindness whenever they could.

BEAUTIFUL CATS AND GORGEOUS CHICKS

It was a hot summer, and they sweated out most of it on long subway rides downtown, where they went to audition for the booking agents. Years later, Duke Ellington's orchestra would celebrate the subway line between Harlem and downtown Manhattan in Billy Strayhorn's signature tune, "Take the A Train."

Originally, real estate developers had planned the Harlem area for the wealthy. The developers had erected brownstone buildings along tree lined streets and wide avenues. But the building boom was followed by the financial crash of '29, that left many dwellings empty. A clever black realtor, Philip Payton, seized the opportunity to buy leases at a low price and then lease apartments to black tenants. New York's African-Americans had first settled around West Thirtieth Street. In 1910, much of the area was demolished to make way for the construction of Pennsylvania Railroad Station, and scores of families found themselves without a place to live. They were delighted to find spacious, affordable new homes in a neighborhood uptown. Though many of the newcomers paid rent, others were able to purchase land, and buildings, here and become landlords in their own right. The reputation of the Big Apple and Harlem also drew African-Americans from southern farmlands and from cities further south and west.

Although housing was not legally segregated in New York, it became so in practice. As more and more black people moved into the Harlem area, the remaining whites moved further north.[2]

Harlem attracted the first crop of college-educated African-Americans and some of the first black artists. Among them were the writers Claude McKay (1891–1948), Countee Cullen (1903–1946), Jean Toomer (1894–1967), Langston Hughes (1902–1967), and Zora Neale Hurston (1903–1960). The painters included Aaron Douglas (1899–1989), Palmer Hayden (1893–1973), and William Henry Johnson (1901–1970). These were people who had traveled and studied abroad, made a name for themselves, and entered a mixed black-and-white artistic community. They bridged the worlds of "uptown" and "downtown." Historians later described this flowering of the arts in 1920s Harlem as an African-American rebirth, and called it the "Harlem Renaissance."

Our three young musicians from Washington, D.C., could hardly have been aware of all this. For the moment, they were outsiders, watching and learning. While they were still hunting for work, two more friends—Arthur Whetsol and Elmer Snowden, had come north to join them. They decided to form a band, under the name of the Washingtonians. Elmer Snowden agreed to take care of the business end of things.

Snowden, on the banjo, was a strong and influential rhythm player. Duke thought Snowden had "a flair for soul, plus ragtime, and a jumping thing that tore us all up."[3] The Washingtonians paid strict attention to their appearance and manners. If anyone showed up looking sloppy or misbehaved, Arthur Whetsol's long face and muttering remarks would soon set him straight.

A musician could pick up some cash and a square meal by playing at "rent parties." Often, people in Harlem raised money for the rent by throwing a party. They would put up signs, cook a pot of rice and beans, and hire a piano player or small band for dancing. Then, the tenants collected money at the door. The musicians wouldn't earn much, but they could fill up on the food.

After-hour nightclubs were yet another source of income. Most clubs closed around two A.M. Patrons who didn't want the party to end could find a few special places that stayed open 'till dawn. Many musicians went to these clubs to unwind and socialize after their own work was done. Frequently, their way of relaxing was to sit in with the local band to jam a few rounds, or to challenge one another to a cutting contest. Besides the fun of trying to outplay one another, there would be tips from customers. For young players, it was a way to meet others in the field, pick up news, and catch up on the latest sounds and techniques.

After some tough weeks, the Washingtonians at last had a stroke of luck. Ada Smith, a fine-looking singer whose bright red hair earned her the nickname "Bricktop," had met the group earlier in Washington and taken a liking to them. Years later, Bricktop would become the proprietor of a well-known Paris nightclub, but at the moment, she was appearing at a Harlem cabaret called Barron's Exclusive Club. She asked the owner, Barron D. Wilkins, to give these boys a chance. Wilkins—another of those beautiful cats who liked to extend a helping hand—actually fired the musicians then working for him and hired the Washingtonians in their place.

Barron's maintained a classy atmosphere, and Duke was pleased to have a steady job; not that he earned a steady income, though. The average nightclub entertainer worked mainly for tips. When a customer enjoyed the show, he might throw ten or twenty dollars' worth of change on the floor. The band would scramble to pick it up and share it, but not every performance brought in the big spenders.

Now that Duke was working, he asked Edna to join him in New York. For the time being, Mercer stayed with his grandparents, to continue school in Washington. When he came to live with his parents during the summer months, he found Harlem rather drab. Unfortunately, his parents' all-night schedule left them little time to spend with their son. Duke and Edna were renting a room in an apartment on Seventh Avenue, with a couch for the boy. When Mercer woke up in the morning, his parents would just be going to bed. While they slept, the boy tiptoed out and walked up to 125th Street to get himself a hot dog or a sardine sandwich. On the way, though, he usually had to fight to hold on to the quarter his parents had left for him. A gang of kids knew when he'd be going out to eat, and as soon as they saw him, they'd jump on him. On days when he couldn't defend his quarter, there would be no breakfast.[4]

Worse yet, however, Mercer couldn't help noticing a certain tension between his parents. His handsome father was surrounded by pretty women—singers, dancers, and showgirls. It was a world of "gorgeous chicks" in scanty costumes. Like his father, Duke was a flirt, a sweet talker, a romancer, and lover of women. Even under the best circumstances, the endless good-time atmosphere of the nightclub was not exactly conducive to family living.

Nor did Edna fit in comfortably with the midnight world of show business. She loved her husband and was devastated by his infidelities. One day they had a terrible showdown, and Edna slashed Duke's cheek with a knife. He carried the scar to the end of his days, but though he was often asked about it, he would never discuss it. Soon afterward, he and Edna separated, and she returned to Washington. But they were never divorced.

Mercer's growing up was not as pleasant as Duke's childhood had been. There were times when the boy resented his charming, sociable, preoccupied father, who spent so much of the day sleeping, composing, or rehearsing. By the time Mercer was eight years old, he sometimes traveled with the band. He called all the musicians "uncle" and grew to like this extended family. Eventually, of course, Mercer won his father's love and respect. As an adult, he became

42

business manager and trumpet player for the Duke Ellington orchestra, and finally became its leader after his father's death.

Actually, the room Mercer remembers sharing with his parents had been chosen with an eye to the future. Duke Ellington wisely cultivated the people who could help him get ahead in show business. A prominent vaudeville team—Leonard Harper and Osceola Blanks owned their apartment at the time. Not only were they successful performers but they also exerted influence in show business. Musical revues featuring black singers and dancers had become an exciting new specialty, and Harper was casting and directing several of these productions. While the Ellingtons were renting his spare room, Harper was asked to produce a show called "Harper's Dixie Revue" for the Hollywood Club, a cabaret at Broadway and Forty-ninth Street.

Once again, Duke Ellington was in the right place at the right time. Harper thought well of him and the band. To their good fortune, the producer picked the Washingtonians to appear in the revue. Moving from Barron's to Times Square was really breaking into the big time. The Great White Way, with its theaters, cabarets, nightclubs, theatrical agents, Tin Pan Alley publishers, and producers' offices, was the very heart of the entertainment world.

CHAPTER FIVE

NIGHTLIFE

In 1920, the sale and manufacture of alcoholic drinks became illegal in the United States under the Eighteenth Amendment passed by Congress. Prohibition was intended to protect the citizens. But World War I, with its anxieties and shortages, had recently ended and an economic boom had followed. Everyone wanted to celebrate, and with extra money to spend, folks were out for a high old time. Usually, this translated into an evening of dancing and drinking. And while drug use was not widespread in the 1920s, illegal use of alcohol became a serious problem.

In the nightclubs that mushroomed everywhere in the 1920s, people could spend an evening with friends, dancing until dawn. A handful of musicians provided the beat, and customers could obtain forbidden "booze" sold "under the counter," or even served in tea or coffee cups to disguise the contents. Customers who wanted a higher grade of liquor brought in their own flasks, concealed in their hip pockets. Frequent police raids added to the excitement, as did the close bear-hug dancing, the sensual, raggy music, and the late-night hours.

Officially, the entertainers and waiters were black, and the clients white. But black musicians would come in quietly during the early morning hours when their own clubs had closed for the night, to talk and have a drink with their buddies in the band. Clubs where segregation by race wasn't taken too seriously were called "black and tans." The music world was one of the first areas of American life where a tentative integration took place.

Young people and their dances were considered crazy and wild by the older population. For the first time in history, young girls cut their hair short and wore their skirts above the knees. Daringly, they rolled down the tops of their flesh-colored silk stockings, so that a bit of bare thigh was exposed when they crossed their legs. Stylish girls were called "flappers" because for a while they flapped around in high rubber galoshes, worn open to look careless and sloppy. In fact, everything seemed to flap about those young women, from their short, beaded dresses and their long strings of pearls to their thin arms and legs when they cavorted on the dance floor.

A dance called the Shimmy, in which people shook like a leaf from head to toe, had come originally from Trinidad and Africa. After it was featured in several Broadway musicals in the early 1920s, it became a ballroom craze. There was also the Mooche, the Sugar, the Shag, and the Suzy Q. The Charleston, with its snappy toes-in-heels-out twists, also originated as an African folk dance, but made its way into white society about 1925. There was also slow, languid dancing in a close embrace, to suit a different mood.

In his memoirs, Duke Ellington makes the nightlife appear sumptuous:

> Nightlife is cut out of a very luxurious, royal-blue bolt of velvet. It sparkles with jewels, and it sparkles in tingling and tinkling tones. Some of its sparkles are more precious than precious stones; others are just splashes of costume jewelry. . . . Nightlife was New York, Chicago, San Francisco, Paris, Berlin; uptown, down-

45

town; Harlem, down South; anywhere where they wore that gorgeous velvet mantle.[1]

On the other hand, big city nightlife had a seamy side as well. Like the drug traffic today, the illegal liquor trade was operated by gangsters. The Hollywood Club was no exception. The gangsters fought bloody wars and defended their turf with armed men who were not above committing murder. But on the whole gangsters tried to keep things smooth on the surface for the customers.

The Hollywood Club was a dark cellar, a hole of a place, with a tiny bandstand tucked in a corner just below the sidewalk, so that the musicians had to bend over in an all-night stoop. Duke's piano stood on the dance floor. Big spenders came in, though, who liked to tear a fifty-dollar note in two and watch the waiters and entertainers scramble for the pieces, or toss one hundred dollars on the floor in fistfuls of quarters. The musicians called these men "Mr. Gunions" because they supposedly had not just millions but gunions and gunions of money to spend.

In those pre-air-conditioning days, stuffy cellars became suffocating in hot weather, causing New York nightclubs to close for the summer months. This gave the Washingtonians a chance to get out of town each year and play in the cooler climate of New England. Meanwhile, the gangsters who owned the club made up for their loss of revenue by frequent, supposedly accidental, fires. After each fire, the owners collected fire insurance and the clubs reopened with new names. Not long after Duke Ellington started working on 49th Street and Broadway, the Hollywood Club became the Kentucky Club.

During the regular season, the Washingtonians played their first show around midnight, and another at two in the morning. The real action, though, started after the second show and went on "as long as the cash register rang."[2] This was the time for other musicians to drop in, after their own jobs were done for the night. They came to listen, and often they would sit in with the band and treat the crowd to a jam session or a cutting contest.

Of these events, Duke later said, "A jam session is like a polite encounter, or an exchange of compliments, but in the old days they had cutting contests where you defended your honor with your instrument."[3]

Once, he remembers, two trumpet players went on cutting each other all night long: "They just happened to have their horns with them. Without them, they would have been like knights walking around without swords or armor."[4]

When the Washingtonians first came to work on Broadway they played a competent kind of "society music." It was functional—rhythmic enough for dancing and served to accompany the singers and chorus girls of the floor show, but this music had little character of its own.

Gradually, the great stride pianists like James P. Johnson and Fats Waller were becoming tops in the black entertainment world. Tastes were changing. Ragtime was losing popularity, giving way to the sound of the blues and the beginnings of jazz. Ragtime passed from the scene by World War I.

Blues, like rags, originated in the black South. Ragtime was instrumental music. Piano players developed it, with the sound of brass marching bands or banjo minstrel shows still ringing in their ears. Blues, on the other hand, had closer kinship to the human voice. In blues, you can hear the cries of street vendors and the long-drawn "hollers" of slavery times when the farm workers sang out to one another across the fields. The blues also has the ring of the revivalist preacher's fiery sermon and the white folks' Protestant church hymns, transformed, in the black churches, to spirituals of passion and lament.

The man who put the blues officially on the map was Alabama-born William Christopher Handy (1873–1958). As a cornet player, bandmaster, and composer, Handy was inspired by the sounds that had surrounded him in childhood. Although the blues did not have one individual creator, Handy was the first to write this kind of music down on paper. Even in his own time, W.C. Handy was known as the "father of the blues." Of all the music he composed, the piece most people remember him for is "St. Louis Blues." Published in 1914, it remains popular to this day.

Blues performers treat a melody the way ragtime treats rhythm. Blues liberates the melody from the exact tones of a scale. The voice or instrument slides freely between tones and semitones, to create the so-called blue notes or bent notes. Blues sometimes comes closer to a wail than to a melody.

In the stuffy offices of "Tin Pan Alley," as the music industry is called, publishers soon realized that this haunting new music could be turned into cash. Some agents would pay as much as fifty dollars outright for an original blues tune. They would add a piano "arrangement" and publish it as sheet music. Occasionally, a blues tune would take off in popularity, and the publisher would make a mint from sales, while the composer who had sold his rights to the song earned nothing.

Duke collaborated with a lyrics-writer, Jo Trent. Once, a producer promised five hundred dollars to Duke and Trent if they could deliver an entire show by the next day. Duke was good at working under pressure. That night, the two of them got down to work and came up with a musical they called *Chocolate Kiddies*. The producer was true to his word, but since he was broke himself, actually pawned his wife's engagement ring to pay them. *Chocolate Kiddies* was not performed in America, but ran for two years in Germany, where it featured two famous black American singers, Josephine Baker and Adelaide Hall.

Just what "jazz" really means and where the name comes from is not certain. One guess is that the term "jazz" is from the French word *chasser*, meaning to hunt or chase. Jazz music evolved from blues and ragtime, plus many other musical influences from Europe and even from South America. Composers and performers, known and unknown, black and white, had a part in its evolution. Some claimed to have played a bigger role than others. Jelly Roll Morton (born Ferdinand Joseph La Menthe, 1885–1941), for example, claimed to have invented jazz as early as 1902. Morton started out playing piano in the Storyville quarter of his native New Orleans, a district of bars and brothels. From the extraordinary piano rolls he recorded later, one can tell that he was an inventive musician who carried ragtime well beyond its origins.

The word "jazz" was first used by two early bands: the Original Dixieland Jazz Band, and King Oliver's Creole Jazz Band in which Louis Armstrong got his start. The slangy, mocking word sounded just right for the brash new music, and the name caught on.

Because most of the players came from "Dixie" (south of the Mason-Dixon line), the earliest jazz was called *Dixieland jazz* by white players, and *creole jazz* by black players. Soon, however, jazz was evolving in new directions, taking on a fuller, more artful sound. The more urgent and excited it sounded, the more it was considered "hot" jazz. From 1923 to 1936 was the period of hot jazz. It had a reputation for being wild and free. Sometimes, when the players got carried away, they would make their instruments wail and growl like human voices singing the blues.

49

To modern ears, used to the megablast decibels of electronic amplifiers, the sound of the Washingtonians at the Kentucky Club would probably have sounded thin and meager. The members were also few in number—five or sometimes six players—partly due to lack of space in the crammed cellar, and partly due to the fact that they had to share their earnings. The smaller the band, the more each player got to take home. The Washingtonians had stuck together and created an identity for the group, at a time when dance bands were still put together for each booking and fired when the work ran out. As a result of their friendship and cooperation, the Washingtonians had name-band integrity.

Actually, a few name bands were already on the scene. The most popular band at the time was led by Paul Whiteman, a professionally trained musician from a white middle-class family, who recognized the power of the new black music. He had the inventiveness and skill to blend jazz with European symphonic arrangements, transmuting ragtime, blues, and Dixieland music into a slicker, smoother-sounding variant he called symphonic jazz. Instead of using the traditional five- or six-man combo, he placed several players in each instrument section, to produce that rich, symphonic effect. He also gave the jazz-band image higher status by calling his group an orchestra.

In 1924, Paul Whiteman made musical history when he commissioned a symphonic work with jazz elements—George Gershwin's "Rhapsody in Blue"— which was performed in New York City's Aeolian Hall. A long composition with a jazz element, performed in a concert hall instead of on a dance floor, was then a daring new experiment.

Duke Ellington conceded that Whiteman deserved to be celebrated as "the King of Jazz." In his memoirs he writes, "No one as yet has come near carrying that title with more certainty and dignity." And he adds that, in spite of his greatness, "Whiteman didn't have a snooty bone in his body."[5] While the Washingtonians played at the Kentucky Club, Whiteman frequently came in after hours. Duke reports that the famous bandleader listened respectfully, spoke encouraging words, and "very discreetly slipped the piano player a fifty-dollar bill."[6]

The three bands dominating the New York dance hall scene were Fletcher Henderson's, Duke Ellington's, and Luís Russell's. However, the group that the Washingtonians most greatly admired and imitated was Fletcher Henderson's band. Its members had excellent musical training and gave a polished performance. What's more, in 1924 Henderson made a lucky new acquisition, the fabulous trumpet player Louis Armstrong who would later become world-famous.

Meanwhile, the Washingtonians struck out in a direction of their own. While Paul Whiteman's band sounded smooth and romantic, Duke strove for a rougher, wilder effect. He was beginning to use the individual sounds of his orchestra members as an artist uses paints and textures. He added a player who could "growl" on his trumpet. A New Orleans native, Bubber Miley, was an experienced blues player, who had accompanied singer Mamie Smith. He knew how to make his trumpet snarl like a jungle animal, or go "wah-wah-wah" like an inconsolable child. To get these effects, he used an old toilet plunger as a mute, which he opened and closed over the mouth of the horn.

With Miley came his friend, trombonist Charlie "Plug" Irvis, who also specialized in strange effects. Irvis's trick was to use a broken trombone mute, and even a crushed tomato can. The audience liked those rough growls and bluesy wails, which were often pub-

51

licized as truly "African," wild, primitive jungle sounds. When Irvis left the band three years later, he was replaced by Joe "Tricky Sam" Nanton, yet another expert with the plunger mute.

The strongest jazz influence on the band, however, arrived with the irresistible clarinet and soprano saxophone playing of Sidney Bechet. He, too, had grown up in New Orleans, the cradle of jazz. From childhood on, Bechet had roamed the alleys and sat in the bars and brothels of Storyville, the "red light district" of New Orleans, soaking up the coarse, hot, local music, until jazz came as naturally to him as his native language.

Bechet was a prickly character who had trouble getting along with people, so he didn't stay long with the Washingtonians. Meanwhile, though, he made his impact. Ellington later remembered the nightly cutting contests between Bechet and Miley:

They would play five or six choruses at a time, and while one was playing, the other would be backstage taking a nip. They were two very colorful gladiators. Often, when Bechet was blowing, he would say, "I'm going to call Goola this time!" Goola was his dog, a big German shepherd. Goola wasn't always there, but he was calling him anyway with a kind of throaty growl."

So it happened that, gradually, the Washingtonians' playing took on a hotter, rougher, more bluesy sound, with a special something of its own. As a result, people no longer came into the club just to dance and drink, but to listen specifically to the Washingtonians.

But although they were developing originality and character, they were not getting any richer. Duke began to feel that it was time to move ahead.

52

When Elmer Snowden had a financial disagreement with the band and quit, Duke saw the opportunity to make a major change. In those days, it was generally accepted that black musicians needed a white manager to make connections for them, find new bookings, handle the difficulties of segregation, and generally introduce the performers to a wider public. In return, the manager would take a hefty cut of the group's earnings, but if he were a real go-getter, he would be worth the cut. Duke, with his shrewd business sense, was willing to make a deal.

The manager they needed soon turned up in the person of short, feisty, cigar-chewing "show biz" expert, Irving Mills. A songwriter in his own right, publisher, singer, and shrewd promoter, Mills saw great possibilities in Ellington and the band, while Ellington, in turn, sensed the promoter's nerve and know-how. Interviewed many years later, Mills recalled, "I heard the band and I knew immediately that this is the band that I want to build up for the best black band in the country."[8]

In 1926, they signed a contract that benefited both parties. Mills was to be the band's manager, Duke its leader. The little gang of inexperienced youngsters who went into the Kentucky Club as the Washingtonians was transformed into Duke Ellington and His Orchestra.

Irving Mills promptly flooded the entertainment industry with high-powered publicity releases: "Primitive rhythms! Weird melodies! Amazing syncopations!" were some of his descriptions of the Ellington style.[9] Mills also had excellent contacts in the recording industry and radio. Under his management, Duke and his men made their first great recordings, including "East St. Louis Toodle-oo," "Creole Love Call," and "Black and Tan Fantasy." For their first radio appearances, one of the small private stations just starting to do business had arranged to broadcast the show from the Kentucky Club. Subscribers could listen to the late-night show and dance at home to the sound of the band.

Duke and Irving Mills, both ambitious for greater fame and profit, thought the time had come to leave the Kentucky Club's cramped basement and head for something better. In the fall of 1927, Harlem's popular and spacious Cotton Club had an opening for a new band. The first group selected had backed out of the job because the pay seemed low for the ten-man band needed for such a large hall. Duke was not put off. He would enlarge his own band, accept the modest salary, and apply. He and his group needed a chance to shine in the spotlight.

As things turned out, Duke had to play a job in Philadelphia the day of the auditions. After spending the whole morning trying to round up extra players to make up the necessary number, he arrived in New York so late that the auditions were almost over. Once again, though, he was in the right place at the right time. As luck would have it, the man who did the hiring was also late that day. It didn't bother him a bit that he had missed all the other auditions, because he took an immediate liking to Duke.

In no time at all, Irving Mills had proved his business talents by signing a contract for Duke Ellington and His Orchestra to move to the Cotton Club. There was only one hitch. The orchestra was under contract to a theater in Philadelphia that would not let it go. Like all the clubs, the Cotton Club was run by a group of gangsters. The story goes that a representative was sent to the theater owner: "Be big about it," said the gangster to the owner, "be big about it, or you'll be dead." And so, in December 1927, Duke Ellington and His Orchestra were back in Harlem—on Lenox Avenue at 143rd Street—opening a new show in a swanky establishment. The show's two big hits, by the way, were called *Dancemania*, and *Jazzmania*, which tells us how wild people were about both dancing and jazz in those days.[10]

Now approaching age thirty, Duke had become a handsome, stylish man. No doubt his elegant manners and expressive speech helped his career. A well-known publicity photo taken at about this time shows him as radiant in white tie and tails, his luminous eyes reminiscent of those of his beautiful mother. In the fashion of the day, his hair is combed back slickly from his high forehead, and he wears a pencil-line moustache.

The magnetic Ellington charm that is evident in this early photo would not fail him for the rest of his life. In a recent TV documentary about Duke, his ability to charm—his charisma—is mentioned again and again. Screenwriter Sid Kuller calls him "the charmer of all time." And his granddaughter Mercedes Ellington fondly recalls: "He was a charming man. . . . He charmed women, he charmed the family, he charmed the musicians."[11]

Yet charm alone was not the secret of Duke's success. He attracted people and kept their loyalty because he drew them along with him into the adventure of music making. Jazz clarinetist Barney Bigard makes this very clear when he writes in his memoirs how he decided to join Duke's orchestra at the Cotton Club. Although Duke offered a lower salary than Bigard was making at his current job, Bigard decided to go with Duke because "the more the man talked, the more I liked him." One reason was that he always used the plural—"Our band," "We can stay there"—and Barney liked that about him from the start. "He thought of a band as a unit and I dug him." Then Bigard adds, "I started that Friday and ended fourteen years later. It must have been my best move in life, I think."[12]

CHAPTER SIX

BREAKING FREE

The Cotton Club is still remembered for its fast dancing and free-spending good time. A film about it, titled *The Cotton Club*, came out in 1991. The club seated about five hundred people, almost three times as many as could fit into the Kentucky Club, and its shows were broadcast, nationally and even internationally, on the radio.

While Duke and the band had been playing downtown, Harlem nightlife had changed. Originally, the local clubs had mainly served a black audience. Now, curious white tourists were coming uptown. A number of so-called "black-and-tans" were opening—black-staffed night-clubs catering mainly to whites. The neighborhood, the floor show, the musicians, and the waiters, were all black. An occasional party of well-to-do African-Americans might be seated unobtrusively in the rear, but most of the customers were white sightseers, playboys, show girls, writers, and artists. Word had spread that uptown the jazz was hot, the dancing fast, and the floor shows spicy. A wad of money would buy all this and bootlegged liquor, too.

The Cotton Club offered all the usual features people expected from late-night entertainment: leggy, barely dressed dancers, illegal booze, and raunchy jokes. In addition, white visitors came because they were fascinated by African-American life.

When holiday-makers went uptown to observe

their dark, intriguing fellow citizens, they paid no attention to the many indignities, illnesses, and poverty that plagued the black community. In those days, before widespread drug-trading, city streets were not yet the scene of violence they are today. Still, the clubs were controlled by gangsters and sold liquor "under the counter." The risk of nightclub-hopping in the wee hours of the morning probably added to the tourists' excitement. Knife fights, shoot-outs, and police raids were not uncommon inside and outside the overheated, smoke-filled, boozy-smelling premises.

Although the Cotton Club's name and decor were based on a Deep South plantation theme, the shows' settings were usually some imaginary African country or tropical island, with jungle plants and palm trees. To accompany the exotic floor shows, Duke experimented with "jungle" sounds designed to imitate the hoots and growls of strange birds and wild animals. Two short films the band made at this time took place in the same kind of tropical never-never land. One was called *Bundle of Blues*. The other, *Black and Tan Fantasy*, was based on Duke's composition of the same name.

As the band played nightly at the Cotton Club to back up the stage show and the dancing, its popularity increased. The biggest boost came from radio, which broadcast across the nation and all the way to England and France, and from the booming record industry. Irving Mills, ever ahead of the game, seemed able to shake recording dates out of his sleeves. The trend was to bigger bands, and Duke had added new members. But he and his sidemen still cut some of their favorite records with a traditional five-man jazz combo.

Mills pressed Duke to compose and advised him to record only his own music. Clever promoter that he was, Mills could tell what would go over with an

audience. In Duke's words, "He went by ear and vibrations. He could feel a song. He'd take a good
lyricist, tell him, 'Now this song needs something right
here,' and the cat would go over it, and it would come
out perfect. He was a clever man."[1]

Mills supported Duke's need to break away from
the Dixieland tradition and strike out on his own.
Seeing that Mills's hunches were so often successful,
Duke felt free to experiment and so create a special
sound for his band, the unique Ellington voice.

Some early records reveal that Duke was finding
intriguing uses for band instruments. The records also
show that Duke and the boys had a sense of humor
and enjoyed their experiments with jungle noises and,
in place of lyrics, weird vocals that sounded like an
exotic foreign language. In "Diga Diga Doo," a 1928
recording, Irving Mills himself can be heard. His voice
is high and a little hoarse, but he sounds jaunty
enough.

Critics have often compared Ellington's music to a
palette of strange, rich, contrasting colors. He picked
his orchestra members for the unique tones they produced and combined their instrumental voices in the
same way that an artist combines paints and textures.
Whenever a new player joined the group, the character of the music changed.

A good example of the developing Ellington sound
can be heard in "East St. Louis Toddle-o," as recorded
for Columbia in 1927. (Later, the spelling of the title
became "Toodle-Oo.") The group obviously had fun
playing this one. Bubber Miley and Joe Nanton really
let go, growling and braying on their horns. Meanwhile, a blues background alternates with dance
rhythms. Henry "Bass" Edwards on tuba adds an
amusing *bloop-bloop*, and the piece ends on a mock
funeral note. "East St. Louis Toddle-Oo" was so pop-

ular that it served as the group's signature tune for several years.

Duke Ellington's first genuinely popular hit, "Black and Tan Fantasy," was also recorded the same year (1927), and with a similar musical tone "palette." The distinctive sound of the orchestra frequently was humorous and eerie at the same time. "The Mooche," for example, recorded in 1928, sounds like a parade of hooting goblins. The instruments seem to be marching in disguise, like mummers in a New Orleans Mardi Gras procession. Each instrument masquerades as something else. One instrument, in particular, is even harder to identify than the rest. A look at the label reveals that it is the voice of Baby Cox wailing and wah-wahing in imitation of a muted horn.[2]

Although these first mature compositions are grounded in ragtime, blues, and jazz, Ellington's voice is unmistakable. Duke's parts would have the players' actual names on them, rather than the name of the instrument, such as second trumpet, etc. Duke drew those special effects from his musicians by encouraging them to flights of fancy all their own. He had a good ear for any striking licks or riffs a player might be trying out. If something pleased him, he would develop it into a short melody and incorporate it into a longer composition.

Often, when some idea came to him on the spur of the moment, on the train or bus, Duke would scribble down the music on any piece of paper that came to hand. Mainly, though, he composed in rehearsal, or just before a recording session. He would direct his sidemen by turns, asking them to repeat, improvise, play a passage slow and sad or brash and peppy, until something beautiful emerged.

Improvisation was essential to jazz, but it meant that many spontaneous performances could not be repeated exactly. Duke's music was more enduring than most. He inspired loyalty in his musicians who remained with the orchestra for years. Certain effects, stored in the players' memories, preserved the orchestra's unique style. If the pieces sounded a little different each time they were performed, this was not a disadvantage. Duke liked the players to express themselves as the spirit happened to move them. But that also meant that his compositions never sounded quite right when they were played by other bands.

One of the first of the new instrumentalists Duke hired when he came to the Cotton Club was clarinetist Barney Bigard, a New Orleans, French-speaking, Creole. Bigard's whole family played clarinet, including his grandfather and great-grandfather. Barney would remain with Duke for fourteen years. Next came Johnny Hodges, nicknamed "Rabbit," who had studied and traveled with the great Sidney Bechet. To hear Johnny Hodges's ravishing alto saxophone, his smooth, long phrases, and swinging rhythms, one would never suspect that he was shy, insecure, and hard to get along with. He could hardly read music, not to mention write down the beautiful melodies that occurred to him. Instead, he would play them to another new member, trombonist Juan Tizol, who was trained to read and write music.

Juan Tizol came to New York from Puerto Rico, where he had obtained a good, traditional music education. His uncle was a famous symphony orchestra conductor in San Juan. In 1929, when the band landed a job playing for the George Gershwin show *Show Girl*, Duke needed someone like Tizol to help him out. Since Duke and his sidemen were shaky readers, they had trouble deciphering the complicated score without Tizol.

Juan stayed with the band for fifteen years and became Ellington's musical right-hand man, transposing Duke's scribbles and rough drafts into parts for each of the instrumentalists. Juan Tizol was not one of the great jazz naturals, but Duke appreciated his pure, classical tone on the trombone and put it to good use.

As for the trumpet section, Duke decided to expand it to a group of three. This gave him the use of a brass choir, and, by adding a trombone, he could create the four-part harmonies and dissonances that were becoming his specialty. Duke's old buddy, trumpet player Arthur Whetsol, returned to the band after he finished medical school.

Meanwhile, though, Bubber Miley, the Washingtonians' first growling horn player, had to be sent packing. Of all the cutups in the band, Bubber was the worst. After the show, he would cruise the after-hours clubs, get drunk, hang out all the next day, and show up for work late, if at all. He would stumble to his seat, dirty and unshaven, and sometimes he would fall asleep in the middle of the program. Duke Ellington seldom demanded strict discipline from his sidemen, for he believed that a free, unregulated life would create a natural and spontaneous quality in their music-playing. Duke himself enjoyed carousing quite a bit in his early years. In later life, though, after he saw that alcohol had destroyed the health of many of his buddies, he stopped drinking almost entirely.

With Bubber Miley, things went from bad to worse. He missed important recording dates and broke all the rules about looking good in front of an audience. When his dress shirt was soiled, he'd rub it all over with talcum powder to make it look white. Finally, Bubber left and went off on his own.

To replace him, Duke took in Charles Melvin "Cootie" Williams. He hired him without having heard or seen him perform, simply on the recommendation that he was "a hell of a trumpet player." Indeed, Cootie turned out to be a winner. He had been brought up in Mobile, Alabama, a city close enough to New Orleans to come under the influence of the jazz cradle. Once, when he was still very small, some grownups took him to a concert and later asked him what he had heard. "Cootie, cootie, cootie," the little fellow sang out, and that's how he got his nickname.

Williams's father, a remarkable man, insisted that all his children take music lessons. Cootie studied classical trumpet, which made him a very solid player. His teacher wanted to keep him away from jazz, so he used to give the boy a slap if he heard him trying any jazzy licks. In spite of this prevention program, Cootie became a jazz trumpeter. He idolized Louis Armstrong, then becoming famous with his band "The Hot Five," and he was strongly influenced by Armstrong's superb musicianship. It took a few weeks for Cootie to realize that he was now expected to produce those throaty growls that had been Bubber Miley's specialty. But with his solid technique, big tone, and natural feel for the swing of jazz, Williams could do just about anything.

The nucleus of the orchestra now formed would remain as such for a long time, to play some of Duke's greatest music. Jazz historian James Lincoln Collier calls this group "the musical instrument with which [Duke Ellington] would create some of the finest jazz ever played and on which he would climb to fame. . . ."[3] Among Duke's most famous recordings of this period were "Mood Indigo" and "Creole Rhapsody."

The orchestra was making good money now, but it also had big expenses. Most of what came in immediately went out again, for salaries, publicity, travel, and the tuxedos and other jaunty uniforms that gave the band its style. Even off the job, Duke liked clothes and surroundings to be of excellent quality.

Still, as soon as Duke was sure of a steady income,

he sent for his mother and father, his sister, Ruth, and his son, Mercer, to make a home for Duke in New York. He had rented a three-bedroom apartment at 381 Edgecombe Avenue in the area nicknamed Sugar Hill, Harlem's most expensive neighborhood.

Mercer had been living in Washington with his mother. Although Duke helped support her, Edna was not in good financial circumstances. Besides, she was depressed by Duke's rejection and sometimes turned to alcohol for comfort. Mercer had spent much time with his grandparents, anyway, so it was only natural that he should move with them to New York.

But the boy was surprised, when he arrived in the Edgecombe Avenue apartment, to find an attractive young woman already living there. Her name was Mildred Dixon, but Duke called her his "sweet Bebe." He had met Mil at the Cotton Club, where she was performing as part of a ballroom dance duo. Mercer describes her as petite, with long, black hair pulled back ballerina-style, delicate features, and lovely dark eyes. Her charm and tact won everyone's respect. Without disloyalty to his mother, Mercer liked Mil immediately, and Ruth, who felt a little estranged at first, soon grew to love her, too. Mercer was upset about the separation of his parents, but he had to face the fact that his beloved father could hardly be called a one-woman man. A number of women friends had come and gone before Mildred, and Mildred, too, with all her charm and diplomacy, would not be the last. Meanwhile, though, she lived and traveled with Duke and the orchestra and got along well with the rest of the family.

The 1920s—the decade of the Jazz Age—were coming to a close, but nobody suspected that prosperity and good times would end. Like almost everyone else, Duke Ellington had invested his savings in stocks and was pleased to watch their market value

go up and up. Then, quite suddenly, on "Black Tuesday," October 29, 1929, the stock market crashed.
Duke's holdings deflated like a punctured balloon and
he was left without a penny, and in sizable debt.

Reflecting on it later, Mercer did not think his father
was greatly upset. All his life, Duke Ellington had a
rather detached attitude toward money. He needed
plenty of it and spent it generously, but he did not
worship it. It came and went, in order to provide daily
comforts and pleasures for its owner and those around
him. In contrast to prominent figures in show business
today, Duke never became fabulously rich. He was
not interested in buying himself a fine house, and felt
no need of yachts, private jets, or even a swimming
pool. His work was his life, and he lived the life he
wanted.

While the stock market crash, and the great economic depression that followed, deprived millions of
people of their jobs and homes, the Ellington family
was able to keep afloat. The orchestra played a number called "Wall Street Wail" that year, and enough
customers crowded onto the nation's dance floors to
maintain the well-known bands. Band member Barney
Bigard later wrote in his autobiography, "We worked
clean through the Depression without even knowing
there was one. I guess we were one of the best-paid,
best-known bands in the U.S.A."[4]

In spite of the Depression, ballroom dancing continued to be a popular pastime right through the thir-
ties and forties. The fox-trot and the tango replaced
the Charleston and the shimmy-shammy, and later
there was the jitterbug.

Dance music was every name band's bread and
butter, and Duke Ellington would play it throughout
his career. In his best work, though, he went beyond
this confining format toward more symphonic music
without obviously danceable rhythms.

Young Edward Kennedy Ellington cuts a dashing figure even at an early age.

Ellington grew up in the midst of a large, warm, and doting family. Duke and his mother, the beautiful Daisy Kennedy Ellington, pictured here, were quite devoted to each other.

W. C. Handy, who composed such classics as "St. Louis Blues" and "Memphis Blues," was often called "the Father of the Blues." A cornet player and bandmaster, Handy wrote the "St. Louis Blues" in 1914, and it continues to be one of the most popular of blues songs today.

Ellington's first music group.

Right:
A handsome, dapper Duke in 1931

Below:
The Fletcher Henderson orchestra, shown here in 1927, was the group most admired by Ellington and the Washingtonians.

From 1927 to 1931, Duke Ellington's orchestra played at the famous Cotton Club. Left to right: Freddy Jenkins, Sam Nanton, Cootie Williams, Harry White, Arthur Whetsol, Sonny Greer, Duke Ellington, Harry Carney, Fred Guy, Johnny Hodges, Wellman Braud, Barney Bigard.

The Cotton Club in Harlem, the section of Manhattan where most blacks lived, was one of the most famous nightclubs in New York City. Tourists from around the world traveled "uptown" to visit the club.

This publicity portrait of Duke was taken in 1933, just before his first European tour. The photographer has captured the jazz performer's glamorous style.

*Duke Ellington and his musicians arrive by train
in Hollywood in 1934 to appear in a movie. On Ellington's
right is Ivie Anderson, the singer with the band.*

In 1933, Duke Ellington, in a white suit with a matching white piano, entertains at the Palladium, the world-famous concert hall in London.

Billy Strayhorn (left) and Duke Ellington (right) composing a piece for the Ellington orchestra.

Above: *In 1943, Duke Ellington, at the piano, with members of his band (left to right), Ray Nance, Rex Stewart, Joe Nanton, Harry Carney, Johnny Hodges, and Sonny Greer. Drummer Sonny Greer began playing with Ellington in the Washingtonians.*

Right:
Johnny Hodges (right) and Al Sears (left) of the Ellington orchestra

Juan Tizol,
a graduate of a
music conservatory
in Puerto Rico,
transcribed many
of the Ellington
orchestra pieces.

Barney Bigard played
with the Ellington band
for fourteen years.

Above:
Band members on tour relax at a card game. From left: Al Sears (with pipe), Shelton Hemphill, Junior Raglin, Django Reinhardt (the French-Gypsy guitarist), Lawrence Brown, Harry Carney, and Johnny Hodges.

Right:
Harry Carney

*Duke reviews a score with the incomparable jazz singer,
Billie Holiday (center) and a music critic (right).*

Two jazz immortals, Duke Ellington and Louis "Satchmo" Armstrong (right), visit backstage during a tribute to Duke Ellington at Madison Square Garden.

Dig that crazy scene, man. The Fifth Avenue Presbyterian Church in New York City is the setting of Duke Ellington's Concert of Sacred Music, performed by his sixteen-piece orchestra and numerous choirs and soloists. The Rev. Bryant M. Kirkland, pastor, welcomes Duke.

The farewell to a musical genius, an American original,
at the Cathedral of St. John the Divine in New York City.
On May 27, 1974, ten to fifteen thousand mourners
paid tribute to Ellington, who had died of lung cancer
on May 24, at the age of seventy-five.

Life was comfortable, although, as Mercer recalls, "Pop" often had trouble paying the rent on time and could hardly keep up with the car installments and the garage bill. His music teachers, too, would remind the boy that they hadn't been paid for his lessons. On the other hand, while unemployed men sold polished apples in the street, Mercer always wore good clothes to school. In fact, when he came to class in well-cut flannel pants and a new turtleneck sweater, he often met with hostility from the other kids. As for Ruth, she had grown into a pretty girl, who loved to go shopping with Mil Dixon and had all the clothes needed to make her the best dressed young girl around.

Mercer found the New York apartment more luxurious than the Washington home he had shared with his mother. He was impressed that there were wall switches for the lights, instead of the pull chains that hung from the ceiling in older houses. He shared a room with his grandfather, J.E., while Ruth shared one with her mother, Daisy. At all hours, the sounds of his father's piano playing drifted through the closed doors. As a special present, Duke had given his mother a swanky car—a sixteen-cylinder, low-riding Pierce-Arrow. J.E. became the official driver for anyone who needed to go places. He drove the car with pride, although once he put a big dent in it when he lost control, on the way to Chicago, while waving a roasted chicken leg at the family in the backseat.

Frequent—almost daily—radio broadcasts from the Cotton Club had spread Duke Ellington's fame from coast to coast. In 1930, the band was asked to appear on a program with the famous French singer Maurice Chevalier at New York's Fulton Theater, and that summer Duke and his group went out west to appear in an Amos 'n' Andy film called *Check and Double Check*.

The movie, part of a comedy series about the lives

of black people, was a hit that gave the Ellington band even greater exposure. Jazz critics were keeping an eye on Duke and often wrote about him. When President Herbert Hoover held a White House reception for prominent black Americans, Duke Ellington was among those invited to attend.

In 1931, Duke's contract with the Cotton Club expired, and he was replaced by the popular Cab Calloway. In the summer, the whole gang went on tour to Chicago, accompanied by Daisy, J.E., Ruth, and Mercer. The engagement was a success, and Mercer had an exciting time. But his father was restless and dissatisfied. He needed more scope and a wider horizon.

Irving Mills thought this over, and then zoomed off in a cloud of cigar smoke to arrange for Duke Ellington and His Orchestra to travel across the ocean to do a tour of England and the European continent.

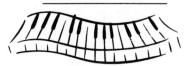

CHAPTER SEVEN

TRIUMPHS AND LOSSES

Even bold people sometimes have fears that are hard to overcome. As a young teenager, Duke had read about the sinking of the ocean liner the *Titanic*. The wild panic on board, and the number of people who drowned, gave him nightmares and left him with a fear of traveling by water. He even felt uneasy on airplanes, and although he eventually became a world traveler, he was never quite comfortable leaving firm ground. His terror of the ocean almost spoiled the triumph of his first international tour. Instead of enjoying the voyage, he tried to forget that he was on board ship by immersing himself in a nonstop card game.

All went well, however. On June 9, 1933, after a week on the high seas, he and the orchestra landed at Southampton, England. A group photo taken on deck of the S.S. *Olympia* shows Duke seated front row center, surrounded by eighteen band members, including two young women—Bessie Dudley, a dancer, and Ivie Anderson, the band's newly hired singer. On either side of Duke are Jack Hylton, the British bandleader, and Irving Mills.[1] Mills and Hylton had worked together on booking the Ellington tour, which included London's foremost entertainment palace, the Palladium.

A crowd of fans had come to meet them, and Barney Bigard recalls that as the band members stepped off the train, the people on the platform recognized them and called to them by name. The musicians' fame had preceded them to England, through radio broadcasts, records, and news photos.

In spite of the band's popularity among jazz fans, an embarrassing situation, typical in those days, arose when the musicians reached London. As the newspaper headlines put it—NO HOTEL FOR A NEGRO BAND. One reporter pretended to seek accommodations for a black man, to see how much chance a black man had of finding a good hotel room in London. "Hopelessly full up," was the answer in one case. In another, "We can put him up for one night if he is well behaved." One desk clerk asked, "Is he very black?"

Things were just as bad in England as at home in the United States. Finally, when Jack Hylton and Irving Mills refused to take "no" for an answer, the Dorchester, one of London's best hotels, found a place for Duke. The others had to accept accommodations in more remote parts of town.

After this unpleasant start, however, the orchestra got on splendidly. The musicians were invited to make an unscheduled appearance at a formal reception in Lord Beaverbrook's London palace. Here, the self-styled Duke from Washington, D.C., met the actual Prince of Wales (the future Duke of Windsor, who briefly held the throne of England as King Edward VIII). Ellington also hobnobbed with George, Duke of Kent (who was later killed in World War II). Both these aristocrats were jazz fans, who enjoyed themselves hugely with the American musicians. Duke gave the Duke of Kent credit for being a passable jazz pianist and claimed they played piano duets together. As for the Prince of Wales, he couldn't wait to try out Sonny Greer's drums, and after he joined the band for a set, Duke complimented him on playing "good hot drums." Plenty of gin liquor was consumed, and after a while the Prince was calling Greer "Sonny," and the drummer was calling the Prince "The Wale."

At the Palladium, the orchestra appeared resplendent in cream-colored suits and shoes, and orange ties and socks. At the Trocadero, where they appeared for two sold-out performances, the musicians wore pearl-gray. Their programs, however, caused a great deal of controversy. The audiences were divided between the jazz purists and the good-time crowd. The purists were disappointed to find that comedians and other entertainers were appearing on the same bill, and complained that Duke had catered to the lowest tastes.

The concert was, indeed, aimed at the popular crowd. Trombonist Lawrence Brown, the band's latest find, whose tone was "rich as chocolate and smooth as velvet,"[2] played "Trees," a sickly-sweet melody that speaks a language quite different from jazz. Then, Ivie Anderson's rendition of "Stormy Weather" had the audience in tears. Finally, people went stomping wild when dancer Bessie Dudley, dressed in little black satin pants, danced the shimmy to the band's red-hot "Rockin' in Rhythm." All this was a departure from Duke's long, inventive jazz compositions, such as "Creole Rhapsody." The real jazz fans deplored his programming. One critic wrote that Duke Ellington had "debased himself."[3]

All the same, the orchestra played all over England for five weeks to happy crowds at dances and concerts. In Liverpool, the Prince of Wales slipped into the audience to hear them once more. Finally, their many friends gave them an emotional send-off when they left to make a short tour of France and Holland. By the time the European tour was over, Duke had acquired a taste for foreign travel. From now on, he would be an international performer.

Travel at home was another matter. Duke had re-

peatedly told Irving Mills, "I won't go South." A tour
through the southern states would have been very
profitable, but for a long time Duke wouldn't hear
of it.

Not only was it difficult to find a place to stay;
everything else was segregated as well. Black people
were still forced to use separate eating places, waiting
rooms, rest rooms, and drinking fountains, as well as
sit in separate sections on buses and trains. When no
segregated facility was available, they were expected
to do without a meal, a drink of water, or use of a
bathroom. The sheer physical discomfort of these conditions was just as bad as the constant humiliation.

The European tour lifted Duke's spirits, though,
and gave him the confidence to attempt a tour through
Texas. This is not to say his racial background was
ignored. But newspapers liked to refer to him as
"dusky," rather than dark-skinned.[4] In Dallas, he
played at black dances and white dances with a rec-
ord-breaking attendance. One review read, "Into the
early hours of Saturday morning, Dallas whites
danced to the music of 'the greatest of jazz bands,' a
Negro orchestra. . . . Our grandfathers would have
given any odds as to the improbability of his appearance."[5]

Having made a hit in Texas, Duke agreed to make
another trip South, this time to New Orleans, birth-
place of so many great jazz musicians. The band received a wonderful welcome in this hospitable and
fun-loving city. Duke always appreciated good food.
Traveling meant trying new kinds of cooking, and
lately he had put on a great deal of unattractive
weight. Later in life, he showed greater discipline, but,
as yet, he wasn't willing to restrain his eating. Among
the delicious local dishes he discovered in New Orleans, the one he couldn't get enough of was Creole

gumbo—a rich stew made with seafood, meat, rice, and vegetables.

His craving for this dish caused him to make a most ungracious exit from New Orleans. Before leaving the city, he had ordered a pail of gumbo to take aboard the train. Rushing to the station, swinging the pail, and thinking of nothing but dipping a spoon into that gumbo, he noticed a big crowd of well-wishers standing on the platform, waiting to see him off. Unshaven, unwashed, rumpled, and toting his fishy-smelling stew, he simply couldn't face his admirers. He made a quick dash around to the back of the train, and planned to come in by the end car. But, panting hard, he reached the last door and found it locked. In a panic now, he pounded and called to be let in. An angry steward peered out and screamed back, "Go away, man, git!" Duke had to do some fast talking to get on board, seconds before the train took off.[6]

By the early 1930s, the Depression was hurting the music business. Sales of records were down, from 150 million a year in the 1920s to 5 million in 1933. Even though Prohibition was repealed in that same year, gang violence continued. Harlem was beset by poverty, riots, and looting that frightened tourists and nightclub-hoppers away. Eventually, even the Cotton Club gave up. It closed its doors in Harlem and re-opened downtown on Broadway.

The long party of the 1920s had ended. Gone were the short, beaded dresses that exposed gartered stocking tops. Young women now wore their hemlines well below the knees. Many young people could no longer afford an evening of dancing. They would instead take in a movie. But it wasn't only young couples who flocked to the movies. Watching the flickering screen was everyone's favorite way to forget reality for a few hours. Theater owners built magnificent movie palaces where they featured a name band as part of the show.

Duke Ellington and His Orchestra was now the foremost black band in the field. Duke and the boys were booked into countless theater shows, making frequent trips across the United States, to California and points in between. Trumpet player Rex Stewart, who began traveling with Ellington in 1935 (after Arthur Whetsol became ill with a brain tumor), remembers being refused hotel service in Tennessee and South Carolina. On such occasions, his buddies took comfort in remembering the support of British royalty. "Well, George likes us," they'd say to one another. "George likes us."[7]

To keep sordid racist incidents to a minimum, Irving Mills made sure the group always traveled in a couple of private railroad cars. One or two cars were Pullmans, for sleeping, with a separate small compartment reserved for Duke. The instruments rode in a baggage car, watched over by a band boy. When the troupe arrived at some destination, their section of the train was pushed to a side track where it stayed until it was time to leave again. In this home-away-from-home, the musicians felt free to snooze, bring in food, share a drink, and, above all, play cards.

Duke had always been friendly with his colleagues in the band. But their number had grown, as had Duke's responsibilities. More and more, he tended to keep to himself. On many a long night, while the boys were drinking, swearing, or snoring, Duke sat up writing and planning music. Sometimes, inspiration came from the movement of the train itself. Barney Bigard recalled those trips:

You know the record, "Daybreak Express"? Well, when we were in the South, we'd travel by train in two Pullmans and a baggage car. Duke would lie there resting and listening to the trains. Those southern engineers could pull a whistle like nobody's business. He would hear how the train clattered over the crossings, and he'd get up and listen to the engine. He'd listen as it pulled out of a station, huffing and puffing, and he'd start building from there. Then, for when it was really rolling, he'd put something that Bechet played into the song. He had the whistles down perfectly, too. [8]

No matter how far Duke Ellington traveled from home, he was never out of touch with his mother. Whenever good accommodations could be arranged, he liked to have her along on trips and in the audience. He sent her flowers and expensive presents, submitted to her peace-making between himself and his women friends, and turned to her for unstinting praise and approval. The only place he had ever called a home of his own was the Harlem apartment occupied by Daisy and J.E. who watched over Ruth and Mercer.

A bitter moment came, in 1934, when doctors informed him that Daisy had advanced cancer. At first, his mother returned to Washington to enter a hospital. Later, she was moved to a treatment facility in Detroit. The family gathered about her there. Duke was in agony at losing his beloved mother and would not leave her bedside. He spent the last three days of her illness with his head on the pillow beside her. She died on May 27, 1935.

Duke was irrational when it came to the funeral arrangements. The huge, weighty iron casket he ordered was made to last forever, and he spent two thousand dollars just on flowers. Losing his mother seemed all but unbearable to him. He wept, brooded, read the Bible, and talked about having no ambition left and no sense of the future. The bottom seemed to have fallen out of everything.

In this despairing mood, he turned to composing, and he created his first long work since "Creole Rhapsody." Inspired by memories of Daisy, he called it "Reminiscing in Tempo." It is a wistful, moody piece twelve minutes long, with complex chords but without a driving jazzy beat. Many Ellington-watchers were disappointed by what they considered an unskilled attempt at symphonic writing. They found it monotonous and rambling. It does, however, express Duke's melancholy mood. In honoring his mother's memory, he instinctively avoided his popular "jungle" sounds and dance-hall rhythms. These aspects of jazz had always been alien to Daisy's religious upbringing and refined tastes.

Certainly, this unusual composition by Duke diverged from the current trend in popular music. Lately, a new sound and a new name had come on the scene—sumptuous, sensuous, danceable swing. Actually, in 1932 Duke had produced a song with the title "It don't mean a thing, if it ain't got that 'swing.' " But it was clarinetist/bandleader Benny Goodman who was winning a name for himself as the King of Swing. Swing was a slicker, smoother, more commercial offshoot of jazz. It was "arranged" by professionals, and played with dash and precision by musicians who frequently had classical training and drew pure, accurate tones from their instruments. Many bands were arranged in sections, with instrumental groups or choirs making a rich, full sound.

Swing would have no truck with the heavy thump-and-drag of early blues, but had an upward gliding, driving beat. Jazz—even the word itself—was considered dated by now, left behind to become primarily of interest to collectors and historians.

New bands, such as those of the Dorsey brothers—Jimmy and Tommy—were coming forward, while some of the older groups went into decline. One group that didn't make it into the swing era was that of Fletcher Henderson, former idol of the Washingtonians. In his new job as Benny Goodman's arranger, though, Henderson contributed greatly to Goodman's success. Duke Ellington himself was having a bumpy ride of it for a while. He was feeling depressed, and his records were not selling well.

Two years after Daisy's death, Duke's father died. While Daisy had always played the role of diplomat and peacekeeper, J.E. was the charmer and prankster. The skills he had learned during his many years as butler and boardinghouse keeper came in handy in the New York household. He took it upon himself to cook and clean, make delicious biscuits, and chauffeur the family around. His heavy drinking, though, and obsessive chasing after women, disrupted his relationship with his wife. Still, these two people had been the family's anchor during the important years when Ruth and Mercer were growing up and Duke worked all night or went on tour.

After the deaths of Daisy and J.E., the household on Edgecombe Avenue broke up altogether. For one thing, Duke had fallen in love again. He had been playing at the new downtown Cotton Club when he was smitten with one of the show girls, beautiful Beatrice Ellis, nicknamed "Evie." She had dark hair, a warm-toned complexion, and long slender legs. Her background was part Spanish, part African-American.

Somehow, Duke just couldn't stay true to any one woman, and Mildred Dixon had tactfully overlooked his infidelities in the past. This time, though, when Duke moved with Evie to a new apartment of their own, Mil could not ignore Duke's latest infatuation. In her quiet way, Mil made no fuss, but simply withdrew.

75

Seeing that their father would not return to Edge-combe Avenue, Ruth and Mercer together also moved to a new apartment. By now, Ruth was a student at Teachers College of Columbia University, and Mercer was in high school. Used to being cared for by their grandparents, the two had few housekeeping skills of their own. They ordered their food from the corner delicatessen, and were always running short of cash when bills had to be paid at the end of the month.

As is usual with people in show business, Duke's income arrived periodically in lump sums, with little money coming in between. His heavy responsibilities often left him broke. All the same, he sent Ruth to study in France during the summer of 1938, and bought Mercer his first car, a Ford convertible. Ruth complained a little that her brother assumed too much control of her life. Even though the trip to France was organized by her college and supervised by two professors, Duke insisted on sending along a seventy-year-old woman as a chaperone.

On the other hand, Mercer believes that the car Duke gave him helped bring the two closer. Duke liked to relax and ride rather than drive, and Mercer took over his grandfather's job of chauffeuring Duke around. This gave them ample time to talk and get to know each other better. Mercer was developing an interest in music. He was starting to compose songs and write lyrics, and was curious about everything that happened in the band.

In spite of his passion for Evie Ellis, Duke was unwilling to divorce his wife Edna whom he continued to support. He and Evie stayed together for so many years, though, that people eventually came to call her "Mrs. Ellington." But even after Edna's death, Evie waited in vain for Duke to marry her. When Duke died many years later, and Evie was very sick herself, she reminisced about having given him thirty-seven years of her life.

The void created by the death of Daisy and J.E. left an affectionate Duke wide open to new attachments. His love affair with Evie, and a new closeness with Mercer and Ruth, partly satisfied his need. Soon, he also found a lifelong friend in the African-American physician, Dr. Arthur C. Logan. Duke had always been worried about illness. Now, after his parents' sickness and deaths he became even more fearful for his health. Perhaps, within this boldly self-confident man, there remained something of the precious only child who had been closely guarded by an anxious mother. Fears and superstitions nagged him, and he never traveled without a large medicine bag of potions and pills. As his biographer James Lincoln Collier has observed, "It is not surprising, then, that when he picked somebody for support, he chose a doctor."[9]

Friends introduced Duke and Dr. Logan to each other in 1937. Logan had grown up on the campus of Tuskegee Institute, where his father was a professor and administrator. He attended integrated private schools in the North, graduated Phi Beta Kappa, and received his medical degree from Columbia University. Later, one of Dr. Logan's many prominent patients would be the Reverend Martin Luther King. Mercer remembers that, on first meeting, his father's nice new doctor friend looked like a white man. He was surprised and pleased when he turned out to be "a brother."

Like Ellington, Dr. Logan was tall, handsome, and distinguished in manner. The two men took to each other right away, and from then on Duke was never out of contact with his friend and personal physician. Dr. Logan was a busy man, dedicated to his medical duties and active in black advocacy groups, poverty programs, and New York City's hospitals. But if Duke, on one of his worldwide tours, felt even slightly unwell, he would call Dr. Logan, and most of the time Dr. Logan would arrive on the next plane.

Yet another new friendship was in store for Duke—a professional association that would produce one of the great music-writing teams in America. In 1939, a young man named Billy Strayhorn arrived in New York with six dollars in his pocket. Brought up in Pittsburgh, where he studied classical music, Strayhorn had gone to see Duke when the Ellington band passed through town. "When you're ready, bring me some things to listen to," Duke had told him. When Strayhorn arrived in Harlem, the band was just finishing an engagement at the Apollo Theatre and getting ready to leave on tour the next morning.

Between shows, Duke listened to the newcomer play some of his compositions. One haunting song, "Lush Life," particularly impressed him. Turning to Mercer, he said, "See that he's taken care of till I get back."[10]

Mercer had recently formed a small band of his own, and he put Billy Strayhorn on piano. Together, they went over some of Duke's numbers and worked on a few songs Mercer was writing. By the time Duke returned to New York, Mercer and Ruth had invited Billy to share their apartment and join the family.

Strayhorn was small and gentle, educated and mannerly. Something lovable about him reminded the band musicians of the baby Sweet Pea in the *Popeye the Sailor* cartoons. The resemblance earned Billy the nickname "Swee' Pea." Originally, Duke had hired Billy Strayhorn to write lyrics for him, but Billy turned out to be an inventive composer as well. In no time, Ellington and Strayhorn were writing music together, a collaboration that was to continue for nearly thirty years. Billy helped Duke make many musical decisions and Duke recalls that when the two would talk, "the whole world would come into focus." People often referred to Strayhorn as Ellington's alter ego, but Duke thought this inaccurate. Duke writes in his memoirs, "Billy Strayhorn was my right arm, my left arm, all the eyes in the back of my head, my brain waves in his head, and his in mine."[11]

CHAPTER EIGHT

MAESTRO ELLINGTON

Inspiration was never a problem for Ellington and Strayhorn. Billy thought inspiration came "from the simplest kind of thing, like watching a bird fly."¹ As for Duke, he'd write about such things as remembering when he was a little boy in bed and hearing a man "whistling on the street outside, his footsteps echoing away."²

A strong, brief memory would just be the start, though. "Then the work begins," Billy told an interviewer. "Oh, goodness! Then you have to sit down and work, and it's *hard*."³ Finding the time for this work was almost the hardest part of all. The band was constantly on the move playing one-nighters and trying to squeeze in rehearsals and recording dates whenever possible.

Duke worked well under pressure, though. More than once, when a new piece was needed for the following day, he would sit up on a bus or train all night and have something ready in the morning. Fired by the presence of Billy Strayhorn, he turned to composing with renewed zest. "Strays," as the family called him, was indeed his right and left arm; he could pick up where Duke left off. Strayhorn, for his part, venerated Ellington and considered him a great teacher. They wrote separately and together. At times it was impossible to tell their writing apart.

From 1940 to 1941 a dispute occurred between

American radio stations and ASCAP, the American Society of Composers, Authors and Publishers. ASCAP makes sure that a radio station pays a fee every time it uses an ASCAP member's musical material. When ASCAP decided to raise its fees, the radio stations rebelled. They formed an organization called Broadcast Music, Incorporated (BMI), and advertised for new works of popular music. They banned the playing of all ASCAP-licensed music on the air.

For bands like Duke Ellington and His Orchestra, this could have been a fatal blow. They had joined ASCAP many years earlier, and their most popular songs had been published and recorded under their names. Now their work wouldn't be heard on the air, and they were in danger of losing their radio audience. New songs had to be written, and quickly, too.

Billy Strayhorn became invaluable. As Billy had only recently come to town, he was not yet an ASCAP member and his music could be aired without fear of reprisal. Encouraged by Duke, the gentle little Swee'Pea proved himself a seething tornado of creativity. He had already written the beautiful "Something to Live For," and "Lush Life." Now he quickly added such winners as "After All," "Chelsea Bridge," "Daydream," and "Raincheck." Most memorably, he wrote the classic "Take the A Train," which became the orchestra's theme song. The A train, as mentioned earlier, was the subway line that led to Harlem. New York City had recently added a D train that also went uptown but veered east, ending in the Bronx and taking unwary riders out of their way. As a regular A-train commuter, Strays was having fun with a song that gives specific directions to the Harlem-bound traveler.

The same year Billy Strayhorn joined the orchestra, Ellington ended his association with Irving Mills. Up to a point, the streetwise, fast-talking promoter had done very well for his client. Mills's tough stance against

81

discrimination had opened up new territory for black musicians. He had booked Ellington into places where no blacks had played before. He was impressed by Duke's stature and style, and always made sure of decent accommodations and acceptable working conditions for him. Above all, he had recognized from the start that Ellington was special or "beyond category," to use an expression Duke liked to apply to anything fine and uncommon that couldn't be fitted easily into a pigeonhole. It was Mills who showed Duke that he could be a composer as well as a piano player and bandleader.

On the other hand, Mills took advantage of Duke. He took credit for every suggestion or word of advice he made about Duke's compositions, and was quick to place his own name next to Ellington's on sheet music and recordings. This allowed him to collect more than double his share of broadcasting and performance fees through ASCAP, since he was paid both as songwriter and as publisher. All the same, Duke appreciated Mills for his knowledge of the music business, and was generous enough to concede that they had both helped each other. Mercer, as the heir to the Ellington estate, later commented with some bitterness that Mills's publishing house retained the rights to valuable songs such as "Mood Indigo," "Solitude," "In a Sentimental Mood," and "Sophisticated Lady." Still, he spoke very much in his father's spirit when he concluded, "There is no point now in debating who profited more from the association, but it's clear that Irving served Ellington well in the formative stages of his career."[4]

On his own now, Duke cut a great many records for the RCA Victor company, whose excellent modern equipment produced a rich, full sound. According to Mercer, the year 1940 was probably the high point of Ellington's career, an exceptionally productive time in which he grossed over one million dollars in income. The two most lasting hits were "Do Nothing Till You Hear from Me," which was a reworking of Duke's "Concerto for Cootie," and "Don't Get Around Much Any More," which grew out of an earlier song called "Never No Lament."

In live performance, the band presented an exciting spectacle. The stage curtain would rise on total darkness, with the band sitting perfectly still. As the first chords washed over the audience, beams of colored light shone on each instrument. But—one seat was empty. The pianist was missing. Where was Ellington? When would he appear? The orchestra played a few numbers, and the suspense heightened. At last, the brightest spotlight shone, and Duke, immaculately tailored, came forward with outstretched arms, bestowing his brilliant smile on each individual in the room.

Ellington would sit down at the piano, give the band directions, and start to play. He picked each number that followed according to the size, composition, and mood of the audience. This part of the program was not prearranged. It depended on Duke's showman's instinct for what sort of music should come next.

The success of these peak years was partly due to two more newcomers—bass player Jimmy Blanton, and tenor saxophonist Ben Webster. Jazz bassists had no important role to play in a band. Originally, the bass had been brought in to replace the banjo as the heart of the rhythm section, because its deep vibrations would set the dance floor trembling. But the player just stood there marking time, having little more to do than pluck a couple of strings.

When Jimmy Blanton came along, however, he astounded everyone with the stirring melodies and complicated rhythms he coaxed from his gigantic instrument. Duke used the bass to the hilt, and he even recorded a series of piano and bass duets with Blanton. Jimmy was barely out of his teens when he joined the group, and his future looked very promising. Sad to say, he was already ill with tuberculosis, and died only three years later.

Ben Webster, the other newcomer, played tenor saxophone. This was a trendy instrument at the time and was increasingly used for playing solos. In slow numbers, Webster's tone was dreamy, but when he let loose he could swing like a joyful demon. Ben knew he was good, and he commanded a high salary. "I always had a yen for Ben," Duke quipped after hearing him play, in 1935. "So as soon as we thought we could afford him, we added him on, which gave us a five-piece saxophone section for the first time."[5]

Looking back at those enchanted years for the Ellington band, it is easy to forget that these were also troubled times. The war that was coming touched on Duke's own history. In 1939, the orchestra had been booked for another European tour to Holland, Belgium, Norway, Sweden, and Denmark. Although Germany was a stop on their way, the group could not play there because of the country's racist laws. The German Fascist government had declared that anyone of African ancestry, together with Jews and Gypsies, was inferior and undesirable—a "contamination" of the pure all-white Aryan race. To eliminate all such people, an extermination program of death camps was put into effect. The concentration camps were hidden in out-of-the-way places to keep the truth from outsiders, but the camps worked with dreadful efficiency. Not until the end of the war did the world discover that six million Jews and thousands of other innocent people had been murdered.

In Germany, the Fascist state condemned jazz as a debased music and did not permit it to be played.

No such official policy existed in America, but racism persisted all the same. In view of the fact that the U.S. might soon be fighting another war, the NAACP pressed hard for the desegregation of the armed forces and for equality of training opportunities. President Franklin D. Roosevelt announced that blacks would have a chance to become officers, attend officers' training schools, and study to become mechanics, pilots, and aviation technicians. Their numbers in the armed forces would be in direct proportion to their numbers in the general population. But regiments would continue to be segregated. The government had decided that mixing black and white personnel might be bad for morale, and "detrimental to the preparation for national defense."[6]

All the same, many young black men were excited about finding themselves in uniform. Mercer Ellington gloated a little over this chance to impress his famous father. Duke had always taken his son's presence for granted and seldom had time to spend with him. "But in 1943," Mercer recalls, "when he saw me in uniform, he realized that I might not be in existence much longer. . . . At that point he began to think of what he could do for me."[7]

Mercer was lucky. As a musician, he ended up in the band and his duties were to give a send-off to soldiers shipping out overseas, and to play for bond drives and other festivities. He enjoyed his time in the service, basking in his father's affectionate pride, and using his army-band experience to plan for a group of his own.

At ease in his own skin and proud of his roots, Duke Ellington was not an angry man. Pleasure in his African-American ancestry had come to him naturally and early, through his large, loving extended family and the thoughtful teaching of his early schooling in Washington, D.C.

Jazz musicians were pioneers in integrating the workplace. White clarinetist Benny Goodman and drummer Gene Krupa had recently broken the color barrier by forming a jazz quartet with black performers Lionel Hampton and Teddy Wilson. To many jazz fans, this signaled the end of Jim Crow laws everywhere. A jazz-loving group of young Hollywood writers came up with the idea of a musical revue, called *Jump for Joy*, that celebrated black history. Duke Ellington joined them in Los Angeles as composer and musical adviser. According to Mercer, Duke didn't write three of the hits for the show until the night before he arrived: "I Got It Bad and That Ain't Good," "Chocolate Shake," and "Brown Skin Gal." *Jump for Joy* opened in 1941 and ran for three months. Its lyrics were witty and provocative—so much so that some of them were considered too political to be left in the show. The songs targeted the American South where segregation was still in full force. One verse goes:

Those southern songs are getting tired
They're sweet, they're beat and uninspired
It's time they were retired
We got news.
Fare thee well, land of cotton
Cotton life is out of style, honey chile
Jump   for   Joy![8]

Jump for Joy had a successful run in Hollywood, but no backer could be found to bring the show to Broadway.

While a musical song-and-dance revue was all very well, Duke had for some time had his eye set on Carnegie Hall. This fine gilt-and-red-plush theater in the heart of New York City was home to the New York Philharmonic Orchestra, and the scene of some of the world's most celebrated classical concerts.

86

For the occasion, Duke was preparing an ambitious new work, a symphony about black history, entitled *Black, Brown and Beige*. Eventually, he found a sponsor in the Russian War Relief Committee. Russia was one of America's allies at the time, which contributed to turning the concert into a brilliant event. Among the celebrities present were First Lady Eleanor Roosevelt, as well as Philharmonic conductor Leopold Stokowski.

Unfortunately, even Ellington fans were disappointed by the event. Although the piece chronicled the historic progress of black people, it seemed to lack invention and musical structure. It did contain some lovely passages, though. The "Black" section, which is based on work songs and spirituals, featured a slow melody, "Come Sunday." Played solo by Johnny Hodges, in his honey-mellow tone, it reminded listeners of a quiet, festive walk to church.

The "Brown" movement, dealing with the joy of Emancipation, also gives a nod to West Indian culture and brings in some Latin rhythms. The final section, "Beige," is about contemporary middle-class Harlem—the aspect of people's lives that outsiders rarely get to know. Blissful ease is conveyed in these lyrics to "Sugar Hill Penthouse": "If you ever sat/ On a beautiful magenta cloud/ Overlooking New York City/ You were on Sugar Hill."

Under the biting remarks of the critics, Duke just shrugged his shoulders, and went to work, cutting and changing, making a shapelier work out of *Black, Brown and Beige*. He performed new versions of it many times, partly under different titles. Without a doubt, short melodies brought out his greatest talent, but at this stage he was proudest of his extended compositions. Eventually, he would write more than thirty of these longer pieces meant for concert performance, many of them, like *Black, Brown and Beige*, rich in fine musical passages threaded together by a unifying theme.

Never mind the critics, however! Duke's courageous leap from pop entertainment to art had landed him in a new realm. Having conducted a symphonic work at Carnegie Hall, he was now one of the exalted people entitled to be called "maestro," which means an eminent composer or conductor of music. He would perform annual concerts at Carnegie Hall for years to come.

While the Carnegie Hall concerts raised Duke's artistic status, his popularity was greatly increased by a series of broadcasts sponsored by the United States Treasury Department to sell war bonds. As a result, *Downbeat* magazine's yearly poll naming the favorite sweet and swing bands showed Duke Ellington moving steadily towards first place, and in 1946 he placed first in both categories.[9]

Success led to further success. Now that the Ellington name was becoming a household word all over America, people wanted to know about the man and his life. In 1946, Barry Ulanov published Duke's first full-scale biography, entitled simply *Duke Ellington*.[10]

Duke was pleased and worried at the same time. It seemed to him that biographies, like statues, were mostly for dead people. The finality of a book about his life made him uneasy. But Ulanov assured him that his achievement ought to be recorded while it was still growing and shaping American music. Family, friends, and band members searched their memories and picture albums to help Ulanov put together an affectionate, informative account of Ellington's life, past and present. It was the first serious book about a jazz musician, and firmly underlined the maestro's status in musical circles.

In 1948, a breakthrough in the music industry gave Duke some technical help with his extended concert pieces. CBS developed the long-playing record, or LP. The records available earlier, the 78 rpm's (rpm meaning "revolutions per minute"), could only play for a few minutes before someone had to get up and turn them over. Now folks could put on an LP and settle back for a half hour of uninterrupted listening. The old "singles" of years ago were becoming valuable collectors' items.

As for the theme of his concert pieces, Ellington was turning more and more toward black history. A popular book, *New World a Comin'* by black writer Roi Ottley inspired the musician to write a piano suite with the same name. The book reviews the story of American blacks and looks forward to greater equality in the future. This same idea had been brewing in Duke's mind, ever since he gave an interview to Hannen Swaffer, a London journalist, back in 1933:

We used to have, in Africa, a "something" we have lost. One day we shall get it again. I am expressing in sound the old days in the jungle, the cruel journey across the sea, and the despair of the landing. And then the days of slavery. I trace the growth of a new spiritual quality and then the days in Harlem and the cities of the States. Then I try to go forward a thousand years. I seek to express the future when, emancipated and transformed, the Negro takes his place, a free being, among the peoples of the world.[11]

CHAPTER NINE

A BEND IN THE RIVER

Duke may have been right when he said that biographies, like monuments, mark an ending. At the time, though, no one could have foreseen the changes waiting just around the corner.

With the end of World War II came the end of the swing era and the big bands. By 1950, the glittering nightclubs were out of business and the dance halls were boarded up. The wartime shortage of players had driven up musicians' salaries and raised the cost of hiring a band. In their heyday, the big bands had featured a lead singer—Frank Sinatra, Dinah Shore, Ella Fitzgerald, and many others had started their careers this way. Now, managers realized that instead of hiring an entire band, they could make more money featuring one singer backed up by a piano.

Meanwhile, the new thrill of television changed America's entertainment habits. Instead of going to the movies or dancing, people got together in one another's living rooms and watched "the tube." One by one, the big movie palaces, where bands had taken the stage between film showings, and ecstatic audiences had shrieked with excitement, closed their doors.

Musical tastes were changing as well. Swing had lost its attraction, and young jazz fans welcomed the witty new sound of bebop. It was dry, dissonant, and sophisticated. It made people laugh with its unroman-

90

tic nonsense lyrics. Above all, one didn't dance to it, one sat and listened. If jazz had prided itself on being "hot," this music was proud of being "cool." Dizzy Gillespie, Charlie Parker, Miles Davis, these were the prophets of the new movement, and by 1950, it looked as if they had erased New Orleans jazz and blues from people's memories.

More changes were still to come. On the popular front, a blue-eyed Mississippi boy devastated the public with his sulky good looks and a churning dark sound compounded of gospel, blues, black work songs, and white country guitar-picking. Elvis Presley made his first commercial recording in 1954 and soon after started touring as "the King of Western Bop" and later as the "King of Rock." Rock music was to dominate the music scene for decades to come.

Some ten years later, four mop-haired guys from working-class England would come along to compete with Presley for the spotlight. Their amusing name, the Beatles, was a copy of the Crickets, the name of an American group. Rebels and sex symbols, Elvis and the Beatles radiated vitality. They looked great in front of the camera, and while they performed for audiences of thousands, it was their TV and film appearances that boosted them to idol status.

Duke's television appearances were never impressive. He needed the physical presence of an audience to be at his best. Also, he was now in middle age. His exhausting schedule, the nights on buses and railroads, the years of hard drinking and smoking, the glaring lights in overheated halls, had dulled his fine features, and left heavy bags under his eyes. He had gained weight, too, from eating meals on the run, snacking on whatever was available, enjoying rich foods. He could eat ice cream by the gallon.

Face to face, though, his air of authority made him ever more attractive. Big, rugged, self-possessed, dressed in stylish, loose-fitting clothes, he was now very much a celebrity. Wherever he went, folks recognized him, spoke to him, and wanted autographs. Onstage, he blew kisses and told the audience: "Love you madly!" He even knew how to say it in other languages. "Ya vas ujasna lublu," he called to the fans who came to hear him in the Soviet Union.

As always, Duke continued to fascinate women and to have innumerable short affairs, while Bea Ellis, the lovely "Evie," waited for him in New York. To Mercer, it sometimes seemed as if his father's numerous adventures showed a certain contempt for women. Only two women in Duke's life had his wholehearted love and respect, Duke's mother and his sister, Ruth.

In the 1940s, Ellington's band had been grossing over a million dollars a year. But Duke liked to spend lavishly and travel with a costly retinue that included his barber. Now that bookings and recordings were scarce, the group floundered—a dinosaur of the big-band years. For a while, he gritted his teeth and kept them all going by paying them out of his ASCAP fees for original compositions. The money from the hard work he had done for all those years went to keep the band afloat.

All the same, morale was low, and discipline at its worst. The musicians' once-fine tuxedos had not only become tattered but created a regimented look that was now entirely out of fashion. The men began playing in ordinary street clothes, often slouching to their seats late and unshaven.

Complaints could be heard about Ellington. It was said that he had often taken the band members' ideas, incorporated them with his own, and published them under his name, a trick he may have learned in his early years with Irving Mills.

The grumbling was especially loud from people like Johnny Hodges, who was indeed a fertile creator in his own right. Yet the musicians had to concede that most of them lacked Ellington's genius for catching the spark of gold in some fleeting musical fragment and shaping it into a beautiful composition.

Independently, none of his musicians could have matched Duke's accomplishment. But the general sense of things falling apart made them ever more dissatisfied. When there was talk of salary cuts, some of the men walked out. Earlier, the band had suffered from the loss of such veteran players as Cootie Williams, Jimmy Blanton, Barney Bigard, and Ben Webster. Now, in 1951, Johnny Hodges left to start a small band of his own, taking Sonny Greer, Al Sears, and Lawrence Brown with him.

Yes, even Sonny Greer, Duke's old Washington buddy, checked out, although Duke remained loyal to his childhood friend and never took him off the payroll. But Sonny was so frequently drunk, late, or absent from work that Duke had already been forced to hire a second drummer as a backup. The truth was that Sonny had lost much of his crisp, driving energy. His health was failing, and he went from job to job, too unreliable to be an asset to anyone.

The departure of so many musicians left great empty holes in the orchestra. Duke hastily replaced the missing sidemen, but though the newcomers were good players, the orchestra was missing that fine-tuning that had once been its glory. As long as there were old-timers who had worked together for years, all went well. But new players tended to flounder, unless they were gifted with unusual inventiveness and a style of their own.

In 1949, a critic in *Downbeat* wrote that the group was "sloppy and disinterested" and should be disbanded.[1] Before long, the renowned Duke Ellington Orchestra was reduced to accepting jobs of last resort such as appearing with the 1955 "Aquacades," a water ballet. This came close to playing vaudeville, and had little to do with jazz or art. The end seemed to be just around the corner.

But giving up had never been part of the Ellington personality. Even though the entertainment world threatened to shut him out, his belief in himself as a serious composer gave him strength. The Carnegie Hall concerts had been annual events until 1950. True, *Black, Brown and Beige* had not found favor with the critics, but Duke liked the format well enough to follow it with *Perfume Suite, Deep South Suite, Liberian Suite,* and *Harlem.* The *Liberian Suite* was commissioned by the African republic of Liberia, to celebrate an anniversary of its founding, by freed American slaves, in 1822. The opening song, "I Like the Sunrise," seems to have had deep significance for Duke. According to Mercer, who conducted the suite after his father's death, it meant "the sunrise of this life and the sunrise of the life to come."[2]

Eventually, faith and persistence were rewarded. Johnny Hodges came back to Duke in 1955. But well before that, the drain of talent from the band was offset by the important new addition, in 1950, of the tenor saxophonist Paul Gonsalves. He was a spirited, swinging player, who had worked with Count Basie and Dizzie Gillespie. His tone was not quite as rich and gutsy as Ben Webster's, but he eventually mastered most of the parts Webster had played. Duke described Gonsalves as quiet, and shy of microphones, but also added, "We call him 'the strolling violins,' because he will take his horn and walk over to a group, or do his whole solo to one child in the audience."[3]

Only one thing was wrong with Gonsalves—he drank to excess and later became hooked on drugs. Stories are told about his falling off his chair during a performance, and once he fell on his face when he stood up to play a solo, and had to be carried out. In spite of these weaknesses, a moment would come when he would save the day for Duke and his team, and make jazz history.

Music festivals were popular at the time, and in 1954, a young promoter who managed a jazz club in Boston came up with the idea of a summer jazz festival. A backer offered a house in Newport, Rhode Island for use for the performance. The beautiful old seaside resort of Newport, with its history as the home of rich and famous summer residents and their magnificent "cottages," added glamor and tone. The Newport Jazz Festival was an instant success.

Would the new, cool sounds at the festival edge out the traditional hot jazz? Would there be room for both? When Ellington was invited to Newport in 1956, he was chosen to open and close the final Saturday night concert. As soon as the first set was over, a series of modernist groups took over the stage. The audience was interested but not enthusiastic. Duke was supposed to come in for a last set that would close the concert at midnight.

While Duke sat around, waiting through the long evening, he started to grumble. He was reminded of the old vaudeville custom of winding down the show with an act of minor importance, and it annoyed him to be treated like some kind of trained-animal act.

Finally, at a quarter to twelve, the stage was free for the group's second turn. It had been a long evening, and the audience was tired. A few people straggled to the exits.

Duke's feathers were ruffled, and his men were not in the happiest mood. But, as usual, his sense of diplomacy was perfect. Instead of blowing his temper, he gave the musicians a boost, thanking them for their help in composing the "Newport Jazz Festival Suite," which they were about to play.

95

At the end of the suite of short numbers, he introduced a piece that he said he had written in Chicago, in 1937, "Diminuendo and Crescendo in Blue." It would feature Paul Gonsalves playing a solo. Gonsalves all but panicked. Surprised and unprepared, he protested that he didn't know the piece and couldn't play it. But Duke persuaded the saxophonist, with a smile, that he could handle it. It was just a bit of blues, after all. The piano would lead him into the solo when the moment came, and bring him out again at the end. "Just get out there and blow your tail off," Ellington told the musician. "You've done it before."[4]

One secret of Duke's genius, as we know, lay in his knack for inspiring people to rise to their best. That night, Gonsalves outdid himself. At the first strains of "Diminuendo and Crescendo in Blue," people sat up. Some who had started to leave, turned back. The sound was neither modern nor traditional jazz, but uniquely Ellington. After the opening by the band, Duke played his piano solo as the signal for Gonsalves to come down front. And soon things really started jumping.

Behind the scenes, hidden from the audience but in sight of the band, sat Jo Jones, the famous drummer with Count Basie, who had played earlier that night. He must have been carried away by it all, because he started beating time with a rolled-up newspaper, possibly to help push the band to an ever-more-driving rhythm.

Before long, as if they couldn't stop themselves, couples jumped up here and there to start jitter-bugging. The "cool" evening was turning "hot." Suddenly electrified, hundreds of people stood up on their chairs to see what was going on. They clapped their hands and stomped. Photographers rushed forward to snap pictures.

Record producer George Avakian, who was working that night, described the scene:

> Halfway through Paul's solo, [the crowd] had become an enormous single, living organism, reacting in waves like huge ripples to the music played before it.[5]

Such was the general frenzy that organizer George Wein became afraid of a riot and repeatedly asked Duke to stop. But Duke, holding both orchestra and audience in the palm of his hand, rode out the full sweetness of his triumph—for twenty-seven choruses.

Only a few years earlier, a critic for *Downbeat* was ready to write off the Ellington band. Now, however, *Downbeat* gave the Newport concert a rave review. Then, not long afterward, Duke's picture appeared on the cover of *Time* magazine. He had turned the corner and entered the annals of history. Whatever might happen in show business next, his name as a jazzman would not be forgotten.

His reputation as a concert composer, however, was not so assured. He kept on writing but the reviews still came in lukewarm. Now the themes of his suites were taking on greater variety. *Such Sweet Thunder*, for example, also known as *The Shakespearean Suite*, was written by Duke and Billy Strayhorn after an appearance at the Stratford Shakespeare Festival in Ontario, Canada. Made up of sketches about characters in several of Shakespeare's plays, the suite contains a prankish section about Puck from *Midsummer Night's Dream*, a playful one about Lady Macbeth, and a jazzy one about the "star-crossed lovers" Romeo and Juliet.

Foreign tours also were an inspiration for many concert pieces. *The Queen's Suite* resulted from a second trip to England. On this occasion, Duke was introduced to Queen Elizabeth II while she stood on a receiving line. He told her that she was even more beautiful than when he had seen her years ago, and she seemed pleased by the compliment. Once again, his friends marveled at his gift for chatting up the ladies, whoever they might be. But Duke genuinely admired Her Majesty and worked hard on the piece he dedicated to her. When it was finished, he made only a single recording, so he could send her a present of something unique.

The U.S. State Department next picked the Ellington band to travel abroad as official "Ambassadors of Good Will." And in 1963 each of the band members endured thirteen different shots and vaccinations and set off on a great new adventure. In Damascus, Duke drank his first Arab coffee and learned about the feasts of Islam. On they traveled to Amman, Jerusalem, Beirut, Kabul. They performed in an ancient Roman amphitheater, shopped the bazaars for silks and brasses, and bought souvenir bibles in the Holy Land. In India, they watched a dance recital and learned all about the sitar and other native instruments. Here, Duke took sick with fever and colic. During his short stay in the hospital, a "friendly little lizard" kept him company. "He stays on the ceiling all the time with a very positive purpose—to eat any flies or insects that might eat me," Duke recalls.[6]

Syria, Jordan, Afghanistan, India, Ceylon, Pakistan, Iraq, Kuwait. Then back home again, via Turkey, Cyprus, Egypt, Greece, Switzerland. Japan came the following year, then Russia, and later, South America. And so it continued.

These were exhilarating, enlightening, exhausting trips. Duke worried about his health, his hygiene, and his diet. He carefully picked his hotel rooms. One room that he refused had a fine view, but the windows were built without glass, so that birds constantly flew in and out. As for eating, Ellington thought it best to stick to his staple diet of nothing but steak. Since steak in those parts of the world was hard to obtain and tough to chew, he tried to make up for it with caviar whenever he could get it.

The audience loved the players and made their heads spin with applause. Concerts were often sold out, and tickets were only obtainable on the black market. When Duke discovered that some local musicians could not get in to hear a performance, he ordered that all musicians be admitted, no matter how little space was available.

Ambassadors held receptions and parties for the orchestra. Never mind that some of the sidemen couldn't hold their liquor and occasionally passed out on the floor. To their permissive boss, they were "just down cats," and everybody loved them.[7]

Indeed, Duke was conscious of his role as goodwill ambassador for the United States. His official duties included giving lectures, news interviews, and press conferences. Sometimes, hostile questioners pushed him hard on race relations in America. Duke remained loyal without sounding insincere. "Everywhere, there are many degrees of haves and have-nots, minorities, majorities, races, creeds, colors, and castes," he said on one occasion. "The United States has a minority problem. Negroes are one of several minority groups, but the basis of the whole problem is economic rather than a matter of color."[8]

When a heckler, nevertheless, continued to question him on the subject, Duke described a recent encounter with the Reverend Martin Luther King. It seems that Ellington was walking down Michigan Avenue in Chicago, when he saw the black civil rights leader riding by in a Cadillac limousine. Ellington waved to him, and Dr. King asked the driver to stop. Two motorcycle policemen in front, and two in back, also had to stop. Then, an attendant jumped out and opened the door for the clergyman, who emerged to shake Duke's hand. "This," Duke told his listener proudly, "is the way the man lives and travels, who is representing that oppressed race, so the standards are not the same every place in the world."

The year was 1963, and Duke Ellington was justifiably proud and confident about the future for black Americans. In 1954 the U.S. Supreme Court, in the case of *Brown* v. *the Board of Education*, had struck down the old "separate but equal doctrine" and ruled that racial segregation of schools is unconstitutional. This decision led to the movement to end the segregation of other public facilities, such as trains, buses, toilets, drinking fountains, and restaurants.

At the time Duke spoke about his meeting with Martin Luther King, he had just published a song celebrating Dr. King's anti-segregation campaign in Birmingham, Alabama. Based on the spiritual "Joshua Fit [Fought] the Battle of Jericho," it was called "King Fit the Battle of Alabam," and Duke had performed it with a large choir in his recent show, *My People*.

Altogether, 1963 was a momentous year in a stirring time. That year, 250,000 people marched on Washington, and the Reverend Martin Luther King mounted the steps of the Lincoln Memorial to tell the world:

_____

I have a dream that one day this nation will rise up and live out the true meaning of its creed: "We hold these truths to be self-evident: that all men are created equal."

_____

CHAPTER TEN

PRAISE GOD AND DANCE

On a cold November evening in 1963, the Ellington band was staying in Ankara, Turkey. They expected to end their tour with Cyprus, Egypt, and Greece. Duke was pleasurably exhausted after greeting throngs of smiling well-wishers at a reception given by the American ambassador. Back in his hotel, he called for a meal to be served in his room. The delicious local food was his latest discovery: stuffed grape leaves, shish kebab, and baklava bathed in honey.

He had just said grace when he received an urgent phone call. A State Department official was downstairs to see him. Minutes later, Duke received the news that President Kennedy had just been assassinated.

The food just sat there and got cold, Duke recalls, and nobody made a move. Out in the streets, the people looked numbed.

For Americans, it was the beginning of a period of violence and upheaval. While some courageously risked their lives in the cause of equal rights and social justice, others felt threatened and angered by the possibility of change. A series of assassinations shocked the entire world. Black activist Malcolm X was shot in 1965. Martin Luther King was gunned down in 1968. That same year, Robert F. Kennedy, the murdered president's brother, was also assassinated.

101

The killings confirmed Ellington's distaste for violence.

In spite of all the violence, the sixties were also a time of great exuberance. A large number of youngsters born soon after World War II were now entering their teens, and their collective energy electrified the entire country. They were enthusiasts, rebels, social critics, and reformers. Their long, flowing hair and unkempt unisex clothes shocked the older generation.

Jobs were plentiful and so was money, and suddenly there was something new to buy and to try: drugs—which were damaging, illegal, dangerous, "cool." Marijuana, for one, had long been around jazz circles, but now it passed into more widespread use. Mercer Ellington remarks humorously that some of the boys in the band tried pot smoking instead of drinking whiskey. It gave them less of a hangover and made them feel comparatively healthy and "constructive."[1] But soon they were back to whiskey, which was more socially acceptable and could be consumed in public places. On the whole, Duke was not strict about his musicians' behavior. He feared that too much discipline would make their playing prim and square. Unfortunately, Paul Gonsalves and Ray Nance were arrested on drug charges while they were in Las Vegas in 1961. For a while, this gave the whole band a bad name, and kept the group from getting bookings in the casino nightclubs.

If America presented a rather frenzied picture to the rest of the world, Duke Ellington's international guest appearances provided a reassuring contrast. By now, he was a sophisticated world traveler. No sooner had he returned from a trip to Japan, than he was off again to attend the 1966 World Festival of Negro Arts in Dakar, Senegal. Next came a stay at a medieval castle in France, to help inaugurate a cultural center, and following that, a tour of South America.

Often, Duke marked these occasions with an original piece of music. He might perform it at the time of the event or write it later on in commemoration of the occasion. The *Far East Suite*, for example, was completed in 1966, three years after his first trip to the Middle East and Japan. Critics consider it one of his most successful pieces, partly because he didn't try to imitate oriental sounds but simply indicated the pleasures he had experienced as a traveler in the East. James Lincoln Collier singles out a section called "Isfahan," after an ancient Iranian city. He calls it vintage Ellington music, "built around a slow, languorous melody played by Johnny Hodges in his sensuous fashion," and adds that "the melody would have made a wonderful song."[2]

Usually, Duke would return from his travels with gifts from his overseas fans. He took pride in the Maori spear, the Russian hockey stick, and the Irish shillelagh he had received. Admirers loaded him down with trinkets, porcelains, fabrics, even artworks. Above all, since he was known to love good food, his hosts and hostesses seldom let him depart without some delicious tidbit. In one place, it might be precious caviar; in another, a homemade apple pie or a box of brownies. He accepted it all with pleasure, being reminded, no doubt, of his Washington childhood when he made the rounds of his relatives and allowed them to stuff him with homemade goodies.

His good appetite was not always a blessing, however. Overeating and drinking cost him his slim figure when he was relatively young. Over the years, he kept gaining until, at one point, he weighed about 260 pounds. As Mercer has it, "He was flabby, and when he sat at the piano, the fat was hanging all over the stool."[3]

It was plain to Duke that many fellow musicians of his generation had ruined their health and shortened their days with hard living, heavy drinking, chain smoking, and indiscriminate eating. Intending to live a long life, he slimmed down, got more rest, and cut down his drinking to almost nothing.

Duke's travels seldom left him much time to spend in New York, where Evie waited for him in their apartment on West End Avenue. She still hoped they would be married some day, although she must have known that Duke was now involved in another long-term love affair. His new companion was Fernanda de Castro Monte, a worldly, good-looking, much-traveled woman, who impressed him with the number of languages she could speak.

In fact, having a home was not important to Duke. He wasn't interested in buying himself a house. Probably, settling down seemed to him about the same as being pinned down. His home was in the concert halls, the dance clubs, the festive receptions in his honor. Wherever he faced an applauding, foot-stomping, adoring crowd he was at home, or at least in his element. From the press he no longer tolerated invasions of his privacy. When reporters took him by surprise or asked impertinent questions, he would turn away, remain silent, or walk out, slamming the door. He disliked having flashbulbs suddenly go off in front of his eyes. Once, when this happened in the middle of a concert, he picked up the glass of Coke he kept on the piano and splashed the photographer with it. By now, he expected people who wanted to interview him to do their homework first. He saw no need to repeat his life story for every nosy newcomer.

Much as he liked to shine in public, he kept his inner self reserved and private. Even his close relatives and the women who loved him rarely caught a glimpse of his deepest feelings. He was at his most comfortable as a public figure.

But what of the thousands of hours he spent in

buses, airplanes, and hotel rooms? The days when he had sat up drinking and playing poker with the cats in the band were now far in the past. These days, he traveled first class, in his own compartment where he could write down ideas, develop a few bars of music into a longer work, or plan certain stage effects. Without being willing to admit it, he was sometimes a bit lonely.

In 1964, he asked Mercer to join the band as manager. The group was going on tour to England, and Duke encouraged Mercer to bring along his horn. The invitation was a mark of love as well as of confidence. In his younger years, Mercer had found his father a little curt and distant, too preoccupied to spend time with him and always forgetting to pay the teachers for his music lessons. Now in his forties, Mercer bore no grudges. He was willing to quit his job as disk jockey for New York's radio station WLIB and take up the challenge of shepherding an undisciplined group of musicians through a foreign concert tour. Bookkeeping and handing out paychecks were the easy aspects of the job. The hardest part was getting some of those individualists into their seats on time. "When I joined the band," he said later, "it paid to be bad. I had to reverse the system."[4]

Closer to his father than ever before, the son now had time to observe him. "He would be sitting in a hotel room, two or three doors from where I was, and he was lonesome," Mercer recalls. "But he couldn't bring himself to say 'Come on down. I'd like to talk.' "[5] Instead, Duke would start some sort of argument or find a reason for Mercer to bring in the account book. Once his son was in the room, Duke would offer him coffee or ginger ale, and draw him into conversation. It pleased Mercer that his father needed him, and from then on they drew still closer.

The elder Ellington was a powerful force, though,

who liked to run the whole show. He knew it, too. After Duke died, Mercer came across a note his father had jotted on a piece of manuscript paper: "No problem. I'm easy to please. I just want to have everybody in the palm of my hand."[6]

Mercer succeeded in remaining independent, and not being overshadowed by his famous father. His sense of humor and his shrewd powers of observation saved him from becoming bitter. He was well aware of his father's weak spots, chief among which were Duke Ellington's private fears and superstitions. For example, whenever Duke sat down to eat in any public place, people immediately rushed over to speak to him, thank him, and press his hand. This created a problem. Finicky about germs to an extreme degree, he didn't like strangers to hang over him or touch his hands while he was eating. His best defense was hotel room-service, which allowed him to dine with only a few favorite people for company.

Some of his other precautions were even less rational. Partly, he was just following show-business tradition when he made sure nobody brought peanuts or a newspaper to a backstage dressing room. But he also thought green and yellow were unlucky colors, disliked black, gray, or brown (he'd been wearing a brown suit the day his mother died), and believed that only blue had lucky properties. Other superstitions haunted him, Mercer reports. You couldn't give someone a knife or sharp-edged instrument because that would cut the bonds of friendship. Nor could you give anyone shoes, socks, or even slippers, because that meant the other person might walk out of your life. He didn't *really* believe you had to throw salt over your left shoulder after you spilled it, but he did it, anyway, just in case. As for the number thirteen, Duke reversed the common belief. For him, thirteen was a lucky number.

These folksy, little rituals to ward off evil never con-
flicted with Duke Ellington's deep religious faith. He
knew the Bible from end to end, and often consulted
it when he felt troubled. He had been baptized in his
mother's church, Nineteenth Street Baptist, in Washington, but his mother had also taken him often to the
church attended by his father's family, John Wesley
A.M.E. (African Methodist Episcopal) Zion. So Duke
was introduced early to peaceful coexistence between
different creeds. In religion, as in music, he refused to
be boxed in by categories. Later, he took great interest
in all forms of religious belief, and made friends
among many men of the cloth, including preachers,
rabbis, and priests.

No wonder Duke was thrilled when, in 1965, the
dean of Grace Cathedral in San Francisco invited him
to play a concert of sacred music there. The newly
completed and splendid Episcopal church on top of
Nob Hill was celebrating the year of its consecration.
Ellington's music for this occasion was not a mass, but
incorporated new versions of existing compositions,
parts of "My People" and "New World a'Comin'."
Johnny Hodges gave a very moving performance of
"Come Sunday." A stirring young gospel singer, Es-
ther Merrill, made her mark in this concert, while Bunny
Briggs leaped and cavorted about in the piece about
David, the biblical character who danced in praise of
the Lord. "Praise God and Dance," is actually the
grand finale of the performance. Writing about his
sacred concerts, Duke tells us to listen to a phrase of
six tones that appears over and over again. He says,
"It symbolizes the six syllables in the first four words of
the Bible, 'In the beginning God,' which is our theme.
We say it many times . . . many ways."[7]

Duke had asked Billy Strayhorn to work with him
on "In the Beginning God," but gentle Swee'Pea was
ill with cancer and was hospitalized for treatment. The

107

two friends spoke on the phone and corresponded. Duke told him he wanted a strong theme of six notes for the opening words. When Strays sent in his suggestions for the piece, four of the six notes he picked were the same as Duke's.

So successful was the first Sacred Concert, that a week later, by public demand Duke concluded a jazz concert at the Monterey Festival with some of the same selections. No stereotyping here! If the music was good, it would be played everywhere. Of course, the popular music scene was changing again, as always. Rock and roll had just about taken over. Even in New York City, where dozens of jazz clubs had flourished earlier, there were now only six,[8] and many jazz writers lamented the end of their favorite music. But overseas, European jazz fans kept things humming, and in America, Duke Ellington and His Orchestra had become an institution.

Indeed, Duke no longer had to rely on clubs. Every kind of concert stage was open to him, now. The summer before his appearances at Grace Cathedral and Monterey, he had played under conductor Arthur Fiedler at Tanglewood, Massachusetts. From there, he went to Lincoln Center in Manhattan, where he premiered an allegory, "The Golden Broom and the Green Apple," written especially for the New York Philharmonic Orchestra. A few months later, he would be at London's Albert Hall, with Cootie Williams and the band, sharing the stage with the London Philharmonic.

Meanwhile, Billy Strayhorn's illness grew worse. Unable to speak or eat, he still kept on writing until he finished "Blood Count," a piece intended to feature Johnny Hodges. When the dreaded news came, one May morning in 1967, Duke was in Reno. Ruth called him by phone, crying, to tell him that Billy had died during the night. "After I hung up the phone," Duke

108

recalls, "I started sniffling and whimpering, crying, banging my head up against the wall." Then he sat down to write a eulogy for his friend. It started, "Poor little Swee'Pea, Billy Strayhorn . . . the biggest human being who ever lived."[9]

A second Sacred Concert followed, a benefit for a drug-rehabilitation program, held in Manhattan's Cathedral of St. John the Divine, on Amsterdam Avenue at 112th Street. More than six thousand people thronged the enormous church—the largest cathedral in the world. Duke liked to think big, and for this televised event, he pulled out all the stops. The augmented band used thirteen horns, and singers Alice Babs and Jimmy McPhail were supported by a smaller vocal group and two choirs, one made up of children, the other of adults. The band's great instrumentalists played solos: Harry Carney, Cootie Williams, Johnny Hodges, Paul Gonsalves, Jimmy Hamilton, and Cat Anderson, and to top it all off, two sets of bright-costumed dancers came bursting down the center aisle. The concert was dedicated to religious faith and had a gospel-and-jazz flavor to it. But it went further in a section where members of the chorus individually shouted "Freedom!" in some seventeen different languages.[10]

A marvelous extravaganza, the Second Sacred Concert was soon repeated, and then given a studio recording. But in spite of all the applause, a few music critics felt let down. Once again, Collier stated the belief that Ellington was still at his best in his shorter pieces. He thought the longer works often relied too much on a glossy surface, perhaps because the composer was unwilling to reveal his deepest feelings.

Indeed, there was another side to Duke's sociable and open-handed nature, a side that kept others at a distance. Few people were permitted really to know him. The exception, perhaps, was his sister, Ruth. The

109

two loved and trusted each other unreservedly, but even Ruth found Edward, as she always called him, somewhat mysterious. When she was young, he had been a stern guardian who didn't want her wearing lipstick or high heels, and who insisted on giving her a special chaperone when she took a study trip to France. He wouldn't let her travel with his band, but thought highly of her capabilities, putting her in charge of the family's music-publishing business, for life.

"He's a paradox," Ruth has said about Edward. "He's the family patriarch, yet he has a childish sensitivity."[11] She shrewdly compares this combination of sternness and sweetness in his personality to the combination of dissonance and pretty melodies in his best music, especially his short pieces. But in his longer works, he kept his real nature under wraps. Expansive as he was on the surface, part of him may have been too strictly controlled. But self-control was also one secret of his success. People often marveled at the way he kept cool under stress, and Dr. Logan praised him as the best disciplined person he'd ever known.

Not surprisingly, then, the autobiography Duke published in 1973 is more like a public performance than a private confession. *Music Is My Mistress* is a big, rich, entertaining book. First, he briefly sketches in his supremely happy childhood. Then, like the practiced master of ceremonies he had become, he turns away from himself to introduce, one by one, his teeming entourage of associates. Originally, he had wanted to write the book in the form of a theatrical production, listing the "cast of characters" or, as playbills often put it in Latin, the *"dramatis personae."* Since jazz musicians in those days used to refer to one another as "cats," Duke's friend and editor Stanley Dance suggested that "cast of cats," or "dramatis *felidae,"* would be more accurate.

When Stanley arrived with his tape recorder, ready to write down what Duke had to say, he had a surprise coming. Duke intended to do all the writing himself. Not that he could spend a year of his life, glued to a desk. As Mercer put it, "The manuscript that eventually materialized was undoubtedly unique. It was written on hotel stationery, table napkins, and menus from all over the world."[12] Stanley's task was to make sense of these scraps and shape them into a whole. Evidently, it was no easy task, for Duke commends Stanley in the book's acknowledgments "for extrasensory perception revealed in his amazing ability to decipher my handwriting."[13]

Duke was pleased with the look of the finished book, a hefty, well-bound volume, illustrated with many photos. But when he heard that the main color on the dust-jacket cover was brown, he blew his stack. Brown! An unlucky color! He would not allow it. At some expense, his publishers printed a second set of covers—this time in blue.

Without exception, Duke's thumbnail sketches of his "cast of cats" are affectionate and generous. Here are the musicians, singers, friends, family members, business partners, doctors, clergymen, even the band boys and barbers, who surrounded him during his long, colorful career. Here, we also find vivid accounts of tours and travels, and philosophical reflections, as in the sections on "Civilization," and "Seeing God."

All the honors and awards Duke had earned prior to the time of publication are set down at the end of the book. The list runs to an amazing ten pages, and ranges from the presidential Medal of Freedom (the highest civilian award in the United States) to more than a dozen honorary doctorates, plus innumerable trophies, plaques, medallions, and distinctions. Among other honors, Duke Ellington received the

111

key to eighteen cities, worldwide, including Amsterdam, Holland; Kingston, Jamaica; and Niigata, Japan.

Although Duke's autobiography reveals little of his innermost feelings, his joyous celebration of the outer life comes through clear as a trumpet call. Where is it more evident than in his charming chapter on "The Taste Buds"? Here we read about his food delights, from homely eggs and bacon, to crabmeat, gumbos, French pâtés, caviar and blini, Swedish shrimp crepes, crème caramel, Danish pastries, Turkish pastries, English candies called poppets, not to mention good wines, champagnes, and many varieties of vodka. And always, when Duke describes enjoying something delicious, he seems to be doing so in the company of others. It is "we" who are tasting the morsel and raising the glass, never only "I."

By the time he had written *Music Is My Mistress*, though, Ellington had put food orgies behind him. With all the world's delicacies at his command, he was sticking to a diet of grapefruit, steak, and black coffee with a little lemon.

Death had stalked the previous decade. Four prominent leaders had been killed before they had reached middle age. Closer to home, there had been the death of Duke's wife, Edna, and that of the much-loved, brilliant, courageous Billy Strayhorn. Ellington, however, was determined to grow very old and was taking every precaution to preserve his health.

Now, at the age of seventy, he continued to reach out and gather ever new harvests of honors and pleasures. His landmark birthday, in 1969, was celebrated by a splendid gala ball, hosted in the White House by the president of the United States, Richard Nixon. A galaxy of jazz performers mingled with other well-wishers, including "priests, canons, pastors, rabbis, university presidents, writers, doctors, lawyers, executives, artists, many of [Duke's] friends and relatives, and, of course, high government officials."[14]

Duke flirted outrageously with the First Lady, so that she looked straight at him and said, "I heard about *you!*" The dancing and music went on until the early morning hours, punctuated by performances by famous musicians. Duke writes, "Can you imagine Billy Eckstine, Lou Rawls, and Joe Williams, all at the mike at the same time, each singing the other's blues?" His favorite recollection, though, was of sitting down at the White House piano with his early sponsor and buddy, Willie "The Lion" Smith: "The big moment for me was when I saw my man, The Lion, playing the President's concert grand, still with his derby on his head!"[15]

In the course of his career, Duke Ellington was received at the White House, both as a performer and a guest, by four presidents. Thus, he hobnobbed not only with Richard Milhous Nixon but also, earlier, with Presidents Harry S. Truman, Dwight D. Eisenhower, and Lyndon Baines Johnson.

Under President Johnson, Duke was invited to the White House nine times. Perhaps his fondest remembrance, though, was of his warm and friendly reception by President Truman. Truman, who could dash off a few popular songs on the piano, dismissed his bodyguard and sat down with Duke in his private study "to talk as one piano player to another." As Duke later put it, "You might have thought we were a couple of cats in a billiard parlor, so informal was our conversation."[16]

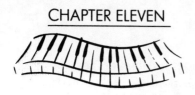

CHAPTER ELEVEN

MEDITATIONS

What better way to commemorate United Nations Day, in October of 1973, than to sponsor a performance of Ellington's Third Sacred Concert. After all, by now Duke and his music had been making people all over the world happy for about half a century.

Under ordinary circumstances, Duke would have been as eager as any youngster for such a brilliant occasion. He was scheduled to perform in London's venerable Gothic cathedral, Westminster Abbey, and his fans in England always welcomed him warmly.

Duke was in ill health, however, and the concert, which was only the start of a hectic six-week tour, took all the strength he could muster. Accustomed to feeling vigorous, he refused to accept the gray-faced stranger he saw in the mirror, or the constant fatigue that weighed so heavily on him. For once, the pills and potions he carried in his medical kit had no effect. Before leaving the States, he hadn't had the time and strength to work out the new piece—his usual way would be to rehearse until he liked what he heard. In London, when the moment came to mount the podium, he almost collapsed. Only a last-minute injection brought him through the ordeal.

Since the orchestra and its leader were highly dependent on each other, it came as no surprise that the players, too, were unprepared for the premiere of a new work. To top it off, Paul Gonsalves relapsed into the drug habit he had been trying to shake. He suffered an epileptic fit at dress rehearsal and had to be put in a hospital. All the same, after half a century of showmanship, Duke could handle just about any catastrophe. He solved the problem by performing an incomplete score.

Miraculously, in spite of all the obstacles, the concert was memorable. Alice Babs's beautiful singing in the section called "Every Man Prays in His Own Language" was answered by a most unusual solo instrument—the recorder. To one critic, the passage had "a curious feel of Renaissance music to it."[1] The old magic, then, the Ellington touch that conjured up strange, subtle tone colors and surprising new effects, had retained its power.

Doctors back home had warned Duke about his poor health. Yet he went right on performing. "Retire to what?" he asked. "I've never had a vacation since I started my career as a musician."[2] So he went ahead, trying to shrug off his illness, pushing himself through the gritty routines of a traveling performer's life: inadequate sleep, unwholesome meals, crowded airports, strange hotels, seedy dressing rooms, the hot, bright lights of the stage. As long as these were offset by great musical moments and the thrill of being one with his audience, it was all worthwhile: "Love you madly!"

Knowing that he was ill, Duke had taken the unusual step of asking Ruth to come to England with him. He wanted to keep his condition secret, though, and refused to confide in his son. Mercer felt puzzled and hurt, afraid of the worst without knowing exactly what it might be. The tension and anxiety between the two men erupted into one of their nastiest quarrels. But the show had to go on. Mercer was playing trumpet in the band, and the two men had to get along as best they could.[3]

After England, the group had scheduled a grueling

trip through some eight European countries, and then on to Africa. In Ethiopia, Emperor Haile Selassie received and honored Duke, and, incidentally, introduced him to the symbol of the Emperor, a lion. In his artless way, Duke often enjoyed great honors and small surprises just about equally. When an airline flying from Copenhagen to Zambia brought in Danish pastries just for him, he was pleased to be able to offer them to the African dignitaries who were greeting him.

On the return trip, a few more dates in England were scheduled, to round out the tour. One of the last concerts took the musicians to Eastbourne, a popular summer resort, now covered by November snow. The musicians arrived tired and shivering, but soon warmed up with a few drinks, comforted by the bright, modern hall and cheered by the fans who had come down from London to hear them. The concert Duke and the band taped that winter night turned out to be their last official recording. Issued by RCA in 1975, the album opens and closes with Duke playing solo. The first number is "The Piano Player" (which is what Ellington liked to call himself in front of an audience), with a backup on bass by Joe Benjamin. This is a brief, cool, witty feat of tickling the ivories, a testimonial to the masters who started him off, back in Frank Holliday's poolroom on Washington's T Street. Although rooted in tradition, it's spiced with a dash of bebop, and uniquely Ellington. The closing piece is "Meditation," from his Second Sacred Concert. As he plays the ravishing autumnal melody, he seems moved to sing along, as if he were performing in solitude. When the playing stops, the final chord is unresolved. It seems to say, Things are not finished, this is not the end. Stanley Dance, jazz writer and Duke's good friend, was moved to ask: "What was in his mind as he played ["Meditation"] that night? Thoughts of farewell? Or memories of the warm welcome he received in England when he first crossed the Atlantic forty years before?"[4]

The first signs of Duke's illness had actually shown up a year earlier when the group was working at the Hilton Hotel in Houston, Texas. Cootie Williams had come down with a chest ailment, and to make sure the others hadn't picked up some sort of infection from him, doctors suggested X rays and emphysema tests for everyone in the band. A new mobile X-ray unit had just been equipped for community service, and doctors at the local health center thought it would be great publicity for Ellington and his men to lead the way in having themselves examined.

The results of the test came as a shock. Most of the men were suffering from emphysema. This disease is common to smokers. It distends the air sacs in the lungs and makes them less efficient in helping the air pass in and out. Coughing, wheezing, and shortness of breath are some of the results. Working night after night in smoky, unventilated places, as the band members had always done, is especially hazardous to the lungs.

The worst news, though, was that two of the men were urged to undergo further tests—Duke Ellington and Harry Carney. Their X rays revealed signs of possible lung cancer. All the same, Duke had boundless faith in the skill of Dr. Arthur Logan. In fact, he had sent Dr. Logan a round-trip ticket to join him in Europe, but for one reason or another the doctor had kept delaying his arrival. Duke was anxious to put himself under his friend's care. Dr. Logan would surely find a way to pull him through.

And then the unthinkable happened. On Sunday, November 25, while the Ellington party was returning from an engagement in Africa to play one more concert in London, Dr. Logan's lifeless body was discov-

117

ered in New York City, lying at the side of the Henry Hudson Parkway. His car was found parked and undamaged on the road above.

Although the death looked like a suicide, not a single person who knew Dr. Logan believed that he had intended to kill himself. His death might have been due to an accident or even murder. According to one theory, he may have been the victim of people who opposed his plan to enlarge Knickerbocker Hospital. The project was going to infringe on some nearby real estate. In any case, the police ran out of leads to follow up, and the circumstances of Dr. Logan's death remain a mystery to this day.

Ruth and Mercer could not bring themselves to tell Duke the dreadful news until the day of Dr. Logan's funeral in New York. That night, Duke cried himself to sleep. "Why did he have to die?" he kept moaning. "Why did he have to die?"[5]

Sick at heart though he was, and deathly ill with cancer besides, Duke still would not take a rest, but kept his engagements whenever he could. In January 1974, he collapsed and entered Columbia Presbyterian Medical Center. But not much could be done for him there, and he was soon discharged. Casting around for help, he inquired about the best doctors and the latest treatments. He put in calls to his West Coast friends, Bing Crosby and Frank Sinatra, whom he greatly respected. Had they any suggestions or remedies he could try? But unfortunately, as Mercer was eventually told, his father's cancer had spread all through his body. For this condition, no treatment was available at that time.

Bea Ellis, better known as Evie Ellington, sat at his bedside in the hospital, and helped care for him at home. But by the time he was back in the hospital for the last time, she herself was suffering from lung cancer. Surgery and hospitalization awaited her, and a solitary, lingering end. She drew close to Mercer during that period, and he responded by giving her a great deal of kindly support.

The flawed performance of the Third Sacred Concert gave Duke no rest, even in his hospital room. In his longing to perfect the piece, he played the cassette recordings over and over again, thinking of changes and trying them out on an electronic keyboard near his bed. He tried to point out improvements to Mercer, or painstakingly noted them down in a handwriting that illness had turned into a large, childlike scrawl.

For Duke's seventy-fifth birthday, Pastor John Gensel planned a Sacred Concert at St. Peter's Lutheran Church in New York City. It was to be Duke's last birthday, and he spent it in his hospital bed, surrounded by a small circle of his closest friends.

When word came that Tyree Glenn and Paul Gonsalves had both died the same week, the news was kept from Duke. Despite Gonsalves' drug lapses and unreliable moments, Duke had loved him for his talent and amusing shenanigans. Now, even this lively cutup was gone. A generation of players, the creators of jazz, were falling like leaves in autumn. Among others, vocalist Adelaide Hall was gone, and Joe Benjamin, who had so recently played bass for Duke's solo in Eastbourne, succumbed to injuries from an auto accident. Duke Ellington, their organizer and leader, was almost the last survivor.

The end came for Duke in the dawn of a spring morning, in the early hours when jazz musicians pack up their instruments after a long night's work. The date was May 24, just a day earlier than the date of his mother's death, back in 1935. His friend Pastor Gensel, the "jazz pastor" of St. Peter's Church, stayed with him almost to the end.

That night, Ellington's body was taken to the Walter B. Cooke funeral parlor on Third Avenue, where, by a strange coincidence, his former band members Gonsalves and Glenn awaited burial. Ellington reposed in an open coffin. On his breast lay the Emperor's Star of Ethiopia, the ribbon of the Legion of Honor, and the Presidential Medal of Freedom. Harry Carney, the Boston boy who had joined the band at seventeen, back in 1927, and had hung on tight ever since, stood mourning over Duke's casket. "This is the worst day of my life," he kept saying. Then, within six months, Carney, too, was dead, as was Quentin Jackson.

Contemplating how many members of the great Duke Ellington Orchestra had passed away, Mercer couldn't help thinking that when his pop reached heaven, he'd find some twenty of his best players already waiting for him there.[6]

Throughout life, Duke had meditated on the world's many religions and philosophies. His views were broadminded, and he regarded various beliefs with a generous, questioning mind. To the surprise of outsiders, who were unaware of his connections to freemasonry, two masonic services were held for him in the funeral parlor.

The people who wanted to talk and write about him came from all walks of life. Blues singer Joe Williams said, "To me he was a messiah. . . . We're a better people for having known Duke Ellington. I thank God he happened in my lifetime."[7] President Richard Nixon praised Duke's "wit, taste, intelligence, and elegance," and concluded, "His memory will live for generations to come in the music with which he enriched his nation."[8] Newspapers the world over praised, and commemorated him. And the *New York Times* writer simply called him "the greatest composer this American society has produced."[9]

On the way to the final service at the Cathedral of St. John the Divine, on Amsterdam Avenue and 112th

Street, several dozen cars drove past some of the places where Duke had spent his early days in New York, including the former site of the Cotton Club. The Harlem streets were lined with people, many of them weeping.

Ten thousand mourners filled the cathedral where Ellington had first presented his Second Sacred Concert. Outside, thousands more stood patiently in the drizzling rain. The Right Reverend Harold Wright led the service, assisted by Pastor Gensel and the Reverend Norman O'Connor. An array of star performers was there to bid their friend a last farewell. Among them were Count Basie, Earl Hines, Benny Goodman, Mary Lou Williams, and many others. Pearl Bailey came as representative for the White House. Music and song filled the hall, reaching a high point with Ella Fitzgerald's beautiful performance of "Solitude."

Stanley Dance, Ellington's longtime family friend, associate, and coauthor, gave the main funeral address. He talked about Duke's passion for liberty, his refusal to be confined by conventions of class, race, color, religion, or musicianship.

Duke's achievements were recognized throughout the world. He was honored by four American presidents, and received honorary degrees from seventeen colleges. Foreign nations, including Ethiopia, France, and Sweden, bestowed high honors on him. His portrait figured on the postage stamps in Togoland, Chad, the United States, and other countries.

Dance also recalled the love Duke Ellington inspired in people from every level of society. Even among nations hostile to one another, he was a force for peace because the countries were united by their common love for him. The number of people Ellington befriended was staggering. Each year, he took care to send out some 4,000 Christmas cards. Because of his nonstop schedule, though, he was liable to send

121

them late. Often they didn't reach people until the spring. The year of Duke's death, the cards arrived just about the time their sender passed away, and so they became a surprising and cherished farewell.

One of the friends who received Duke's last Christmas card—TV host Alistair Cooke—described it to the mourners at the funeral. Printed in blue, Duke's favorite color, the card showed the words LOVE and GOD set in the shape of a cross, with the letter "O" linking them in the center.

At the end of the ceremony, the lovely voice of Alice Babs and the tones of Johnny Hodges's saxophone filled the cathedral, in a recording of themes from the Second Sacred Concert. The great man's haunting music enveloped the mourners while his white copper coffin was slowly carried down the aisle toward the exit.

Duke Ellington was laid to rest next to his mother and father at Woodlawn Cemetery in the Bronx. Bea Ellis, Duke's longtime first lady, his loyal Evie, lies beside him. The family grave can be found in the cemetery's Wildrose section. At the corner made by Heather and Knollwood avenues, stands a fine old linden tree. On each side of it, a tapered, white stone cross bears the inscription "The Lord Is My Shepherd." Three matching stone tablets are set in the ground at the base of the tree. The center one reads:

"Duke"
Edward Kennedy Ellington
1899 . . . 1974

The long, creative and eventful life of this great American ran parallel to the first three quarters of the twentieth century. He left behind a very different world from the one he entered. Along the way, he lived through two world wars, the Great Depression, the wars in

Korea and Vietnam, the years of Prohibition, and the age of drugs. The assassinations of John F. Kennedy, Robert Kennedy, Malcolm X, and Martin Luther King all occurred within five short years during Duke's lifetime. He experienced the civil-rights struggle and the end of formal segregation in the South. During his professional career, musical fashions ran from the waltz to ragtime, to blues, jazz, swing, bebop, rock and roll, and beyond. Musical tastes changed from sweet, to hot, to cool.

When Ellington was a child, electric lights were not yet in common use. Nor did people have telephones, radios, moving pictures, automobiles, airplanes, record and cassette players, hi-fi, or television sets. Scientists had not yet split the atom, or produced the atomic bomb.

As new media developed, Duke and other musical entertainers were able to bring their art to a much wider public. Similarly, modern transportation enabled them to travel farther, faster, and more frequently than was possible before. At the same time, while technology made daily living easier for many people, it changed the look of the countryside and cities, and threatened permanent harm to planet earth.

As for the social position of African-Americans, many changes occurred during those seventy-five years of Duke's life. But a great deal of work still lay ahead. Ellington himself contributed to the civil-rights struggle in his own medium, which was music. As Stanley Dance points out, the musician expressed it in *Jump for Joy* in 1941, in *The Deep South Suite* in 1946, and in *My People* in 1963. "Long before black was officially beautiful—in 1928, to be precise—he had written *Black Beauty*. . . . And with *Black, Brown and Beige* . . . he proudly delineated the black contribution to American history."[10]

Sometimes, the renown of famous people loses its

123

brilliance after their death. This has not happened with Duke Ellington. His name is still known in every country. The New York chapter of the Duke Ellington Society, founded in 1959, meets every month at St. Peter's Church on Lexington Avenue. It sponsors concerts, lectures, and yearly international conferences. In 1986, the United States Postal Service honored Duke Ellington with a commemorative stamp that has become a collector's item. It shows the pensive profile of Duke against a background of black and white piano keys.

Recently, the public broadcasting system aired the hour-long documentary, *Duke Ellington: Reminiscing in Tempo*.[11] Dedicated to Ruth Ellington and narrated by civil rights leader Julian Bond, this wonderful show is rich in footage of Duke in action and features music from dozens of his greatest works. Numerous friends, relatives, and former associates appear in the production, among them Mercer, Marian Logan (the widow of Duke's beloved friend and doctor), and Duke's charming granddaughter, dancer Mercedes Ellington.

For scholars of Ellington history, the music library of North Texas State University has a large collection of books, tapes, and recordings. The bulk of Ellington's manuscripts and scores can be found at the Smithsonian Institution's American History Archives Center in Washington, D.C.

In 1991, New York's Lincoln Center for the Performing Arts created the "Jazz at Lincoln Center" series, including a Lincoln Center Jazz Orchestra, under the direction of trumpet virtuoso Wynton Marsalis. It seemed only fitting to launch the series with an extensive concert tour concentrating mainly on Duke Ellington. Because some of Ellington's music was recorded without having been written down, the newly formed organization, which is also a teaching institution, has done a scholarly job of creating readable transcripts from the recordings. From now on, these compositions will be more widely available to other players.

To celebrate the new jazz series, Lincoln Center presented a gala Ellington night, co-hosted by Bill Cosby. The evening's theme was "Riding on the Moon and Dancing With the Stars," from the title of a 1939 Ellington/Johnny Hodges collaboration. Those who were present at the benefit that night were reminded of the heyday of Duke's big band. Dancing and listening to the thrilling music, they felt that magic spell again—the sparkle, the glamor, the warmth that was Duke Ellington.

NOTES

CHAPTER ONE

1. Edward Kennedy Ellington, *Music Is My Mistress* (Garden City, N.Y.: Doubleday, 1973), p. 309.
2. Ibid., pp. 337–39.
3. Louis Bellson, quoted in Derek Jewell, *Duke: A Portrait of Duke Ellington* (New York: W.W. Norton, 1977), p. 233.
4. *Jet*, June 13, 1974, Duke Ellington Commemorative Issue, p. 54.
5. The *New York Times*, May 25, 1974, p. 1.
6. *Jet*, p. 54.

CHAPTER TWO

1. Edward Kennedy Ellington, *Music Is My Mistress* (Garden City, N.Y.: Doubleday, 1973), p. 15.
2. Ibid., p. 12.
3. Ibid., p. 12.
4. James Lincoln Collier, *Duke Ellington* (New York: Oxford Univ. Press, 1987), p. 10.
5. Ellington, p. 10.

6. *Jet*, June 13, 1974, Duke Ellington Commemorative Issue, p. 54.
7. Peter M. Bergman, *The Negro in America: The Chronological History* (New York: Harper & Row, 1969), p. 328.
8. Ibid.
9. Ellington, p. 17.
10. Ibid., p. 8.
11. *Jet*, p. 26.

CHAPTER THREE

1. Edward Kennedy Ellington, *Music Is My Mistress* (Garden City, N.Y.: Doubleday, 1973), p. 20.
2. James Lincoln Collier, *The Making of Jazz* (New York: Oxford University Press, 1987), p. 44.
3. Ellington, p. 20.
4. Ibid., p. 28.
5. Derek Jewell, *Duke: A Portrait of Duke Ellington* (New York: W.W. Norton, 1977), p. 30.
6. Ellington, p. 31.
7. Collier, p. 26.
8. Ellington, p. 299.
9. Ibid., p. 54.
10. Ibid., p. 53.
11. Ibid., p. 35.
12. Ibid., p. 36.
13. Ibid., p. 37.

CHAPTER FOUR

1. Edward Kennedy Ellington, *Music Is My Mistress* (Garden City, N.Y.: Doubleday, 1973), p. 69.
2. Brendan Gill, "On Astor Row," *The New Yorker*, November 2, 1992, p. 52.
3. Edward Kennedy Ellington, p. 53.

NOTES

4. Mercer Ellington, *Duke Ellington in Person: An Intimate Memoir* (Boston: Houghton Mifflin, 1978), p. 17.

CHAPTER FIVE

1. Edward Kennedy Ellington, *Music Is My Mistress* (Garden City, N.Y.: Doubleday, 1973), p. 63.
2. Ibid., p. 103.
3. Ibid., p. 466.
4. Ibid., p. 466.
5. Ibid., p. 103.
6. Ibid., p. 103.
7. Ibid., p. 47.
8. Transcript: "Duke Ellington: Reminiscing in Tempo," *The American Experience*, WGBH-TV, WNET-TV Show #408.
9. *Irving Mills Presents Duke Ellington*, publicity brochure, The Schomburg Center for Research in Black Culture, unpaged.
10. Barry Ulanov, *Duke Ellington* (New York: Creative Age Press, 1946), p. 70.
11. "Duke Ellington: Reminiscing in Tempo."
12. Barney Bigard, *With Louis and the Duke* (New York: Oxford Univ. Press, 1986), p. 45.

CHAPTER SIX

1. Ellington, *Music Is My Mistress* (Garden City, N.Y.: Doubleday, 1973), p. 77.
2. These recordings can be heard on *The Complete Duke Ellington*, Volume 1, 1925–1928, series *Aimez-vous le Jazz?*, 29, CBS #67264.
3. James Lincoln Collier, *Duke Ellington* (New York: Oxford Univ. Press, 1987), p. 93.
4. Barney Bigard, *With Louis and the Duke* (New York: Oxford Univ. Press, 1986), p. 52.

NOTES

CHAPTER SEVEN

1. Edward Kennedy Ellington, *Music Is My Mistress* (Garden City, N.Y.: Doubleday, 1973), p. 84.
2. James Lincoln Collier, *Duke Ellington* (New York: Oxford Univ. Press, 1987), p. 128.
3. Writer Laurie Lee, as quoted in Derek Jewell, *Duke: A Portrait of Duke Ellington* (New York: W.W. Norton, 1977), p. 54.
4. Barry Ulanov, *Duke Ellington* (New York: Creative Age Press, 1946), p. 154.
5. Ibid., p. 155.
6. Collier, p. 132.
7. Kingsley Amis, *Memoirs* (New York: Summit Books, 1991), p. 68.
8. Stanley Dance, *The World of Duke Ellington* (New York: Charles Scribner's, 1970), p. 85.
9. Collier, p. 177.
10. Mercer Ellington, *Duke Ellington In Person: An Intimate Memoir* (Boston: Houghton Mifflin, 1978), p. 80.
11. Edward Kennedy Ellington, p. 156.

CHAPTER EIGHT

1. Stanley Dance, *The World of Duke Ellington* (New York: Charles Scribner's, 1970), p. 29.
2. Derek Jewell, *Duke: A Portrait of Duke Ellington* (New York: W.W. Norton, 1977), p. 66.
3. Dance, p. 29.
4. Mercer Ellington, *Duke Ellington In Person: An Intimate Memoir* (Boston: Houghton Mifflin, 1978), p. 82.
5. Edward Kennedy Ellington, *Music Is My Mistress* (Garden City, N.Y.: Doubleday, 1973), p. 163.

130

6. Peter M. Bergman, *The Negro in America: The Chronological History* (New York: Harper & Row, 1969), p. 490.
7. Mercer Ellington, p. 98.
8. Transcript: "Duke Ellington: Reminiscing in Tempo," *The American Experience*, WNET-TV & WGBH-TV, Show #408.
9. James Lincoln Collier, *Duke Ellington* (New York: Oxford Univ. Press, 1987), p. 219.
10. Barry Ulanov, *Duke Ellington* (New York: Creative Age Press, 1946), p. 10.
11. Hannen Swaffer, the *Daily Herald*, London, 1933, p. 52.

CHAPTER NINE

1. *Downbeat*, June 17, 1949, as quoted by James Lincoln Collier, p. 255.
2. Mercer Ellington, *Duke Ellington In Person: An Intimate Memoir* (Boston: Houghton Mifflin, 1978), p. 96.
3. Edward Kennedy Ellington, *Music Is My Mistress* (Garden City, N.Y.: Doubleday, 1973), p. 221.
4. James Lincoln Collier, *Duke Ellington* (New York: Oxford Univ. Press, 1987), p. 225.
5. Liner notes, "Ellington at Newport," Columbia Records #8648.
6. Edward Kennedy Ellington, p. 314.
7. Ibid., p. 312.
8. Ibid., p. 308.

CHAPTER TEN

1. Mercer Ellington, *Duke Ellington In Person: An Intimate Memoir* (Boston: Houghton Mifflin, 1978), p. 151.

2. James Lincoln Collier, *Duke Ellington* (New York: Oxford Univ. Press, 1987), p. 288.
3. Mercer Ellington, p. 151.
4. Ibid., p. 139.
5. Ibid., p. 150.
6. Ibid., p. 210.
7. Edward Kennedy Ellington, *Music Is My Mistress* (Garden City, N.Y.: Doubleday, 1973), pp. 262–63.
8. Collier, p. 271.
9. Edward Kennedy Ellington, p. 159.
10. Stanley Dance, *The World of Duke Ellington* (New York: Charles Scribners, 1970), p. 260.
11. Ruth Ellington, Audiotape of Duke Ellington Jazz Society dinner, 1960, the Schomburg Center for Research in Black Culture.
12. Mercer Ellington, p. 171.
13. Edward Kennedy Ellington, *see* Acknowledgments.
14. Ibid., p. 428.
15. Ibid.
16. Ibid., pp. 432–33.

CHAPTER ELEVEN

1. James Lincoln Collier, *Duke Ellington* (New York: Oxford Univ. Press, 1987), p. 297.
2. Edward Kennedy Ellington, *Music Is My Mistress* (Garden City, N.Y.: Doubleday, 1973), p. 438.
3. Mercer Ellington, *Duke Ellington In Person: An Intimate Memoir* (Boston: Houghton Mifflin, 1978), p. 208.
4. Stanley Dance, Liner notes, *Duke Ellington's Eastbourne Performance*, RCA Records, New York, 1975.
5. Mercer Ellington, p. 198.

6. Ibid., p. 208.
7. Derek Jewell, *Duke: A Portrait of Duke Ellington* (New York: W.W. Norton, 1977), pp. 230–32.
8. Ibid.
9. Ibid.
10. Stanley Dance, quoted in Mercer Ellington, p. 216.
11. *The American Experience*, WGBH-TV, WNET-TV, Show #408.

GLOSSARY

Arranger: A musician who adapts a composition to a particular style of performance through voices or instruments.

Bop (or bebop): An early form of modern jazz developed in the 1940s, notable for its chromatic and dissonant harmonies and its complex rhythms, which often obscure the melody line.

Cadenza: An elaborate flourish or showy musical passage, often improvised and played by an unaccompanied instrument during an orchestra piece.

Chromatic scale: A musical scale progressing entirely by halftones, with thirteen tones to the octave.

Honky-tonk: (slang) A noisy, disreputable nightclub or dance hall.

Mute: A device placed in the bell of a brass instrument to soften or muffle its tone.

Ragtime: A type of American music especially popular between the years 1890 and 1915, which was characterized by strong syncopation in the melody and accompanied in strict two-four time.

134

Rhythm and blues: A music popular with urban blacks, which features a strong, repetitive beat and simple melodies. In the 1950s, a commercialized form of rhythm and blues developed into rock-and-roll.

Riff: A melodic phrase, often constantly repeated, which forms an accompaniment for a jazz soloist. *Riffing* by the brass or woodwind sections was a basic feature of the Big Band era.

Scat singing: Jazz singing in which meaningless syllables are improvised to take the place of words and often to imitate the sounds of instruments.

Syncopation: A shifting of the normal accent in musical rhythm, usually by stressing beats which are normally unaccented (also called counterpoint).

Vibrato: A pulsating effect produced by the rapid alternation of a musical tone with a slight variation in pitch.

BIBLIOGRAPHY

Amis, Kingsley. *Memoirs.* New York: Summit Books, 1991.

Bigard, Barney. *With Louis and the Duke.* New York: Oxford University Press, 1986.

Brown, Gene. *Duke Ellington, Genius: The Artist and the Process.* Englewood Cliffs, N.J.: Silver Burdett Press, 1990.

Collier, James Lincoln. *Duke Ellington.* New York: Oxford University Press, 1987.

Dance, Stanley. *The World of Duke Ellington.* New York: Charles Scribners, 1970.

"Duke Ellington Commemorative Issue." *Jet.* June 13, 1974.

Ellington, Edward Kennedy. *Music Is My Mistress.* Garden City, N.Y.: Doubleday, 1973.

Ellington, Mercer. *Duke Ellington In Person: An Intimate Memoir.* Boston: Houghton Mifflin, 1978.

George, Don. *Sweet Man: The Real Duke Ellington.* New York: Putnam, 1981.

Gill, Brendan. "On Astor Row." *The New Yorker* (November 2, 1992): 51–54.

Irving Mills Presents Duke Ellington. Publicity Brochure, Schomburg Center for Research in Black Culture.

BIBLIOGRAPHY

Jewell, Derek. *Duke: A Portrait of Duke Ellington.* New York: W.W. Norton, 1977.

Lewis, David Levering. *When Harlem Was In Vogue.* New York: Knopf, 1981.

Rattenburg, Ken. *Duke Ellington: Jazz Composer.* New Haven, Conn.: Yale Univ. Press, 1990.

Schiffman, Jack. *Harlem Heyday: A Pictorial History of Modern Black Show Business.* Buffalo, N.Y.: Prometheus Books, 1984.

Schoener, Allon, ed. *Harlem On My Mind: Cultural Capital of Black America, 1900–1986.* New York: Random House, 1986.

Ulanov, Barry. *Duke Ellington.* New York: Creative Age Press, 1946.

REFERENCE WORKS

Afro American Encyclopedia. North Miami, Fla.: Educational Book Publishers, 1974.

Encyclopedia of Black America. W. Augustus Low, ed. New York: McGraw-Hill, 1981.

Encyclopedia of Jazz. Leonard Feather, ed., rev. ed. New York: Horizon Press, 1960.

In Black and White: A Guide to Magazine Articles, Newspaper Articles, and Books Concerning More Than 15,000 Black Individuals and Groups. Mary Mace Spradling, ed. 3d ed. Detroit: Gale Research Center, 1980.

The New Grove Dictionary of Jazz, Barry Kernfeld, ed. New York: Macmillan, 1988.

The New Grove Dictionary of Music and Musicians. Stanley Sadie, ed. New York: Macmillan, 1980.

Reference Library of Black America. Harry A. Ploski, ed. Afro American Press, 1990.

Who's Who of Jazz: Storyville to Swing Street. John Chilton, ed. Philadelphia: Chilton Book Co., 1972.

BIBLIOGRAPHY

ORGANIZATIONS

The Duke Ellington Society, P.O. Box 31, Church Street Station, New York, NY 10008-0031.

Schomburg Center for Research in Black Culture, The New York Public Library, 515 Malcolm X Blvd., New York, N.Y. 10037-1801. Recorded history, courtesy of the Department of Moving Image and Recorded Sound, Schomburg.

Spingarn Research Center, Howard University, Washington, D.C. 20059.

Major collections of Ellington materials are available at the music library of North Texas State University, and the Smithsonian Institution's Archive Center, Washington, D.C.

FILMS

In the course of his career, Duke Ellington appeared with his orchestra in a number of short and long films, or contributed scores and music to the productions. Here is a partial listing:

1929—Band appeared in short film, *Black and Tan Fantasy.*
1930—Band appeared in short film, *Check and Double Check.*
1934—Band appeared in short films, *Belle of the Nineties* and *Murder at the Vanities.*
1936—Ellington contributed music to the Marx Brothers' *A Day at the Races* (appearance by Ivie Anderson).
1942—Band appeared in *Cabin in the Sky,* also featuring Lena Horne.

138

BIBLIOGRAPHY

1959—Ellington composed full-length film score, performed by orchestra, for Otto Preminger's *Anatomy of a Murder.*
1960—Ellington wrote and recorded music for French film, *Paris Blues.*

VIDEOTAPES

"Duke Ellington: Reminiscing in Tempo." *The American Experience.* WGBH-TV, WNET-TV Show #408.
For information about buying or renting this videocassette, contact: PBS Video, 1320 Braddock Place, Alexandria, VA (or call: 1-800-424-7963).
For printed transcript, write: Journal Graphics, Inc., 1535 Grant Street, Denver, CO 80203.

AUDIOTAPE

Ruth Ellington, Audiotape of Duke Ellington Jazz Society dinner, 1960, the Schomburg Center for Research in Black Culture.

RECORDING

The Complete Duke Ellington, Volume 1, 1925–1928, series *Aimez-vous le Jazz?* 29, CBS #67264.

INDEX

INDEX